# FROM TRASH
# TO TREASURE

# FROM TRASH TO TREASURE

*God's Redemptive Power for*
*Restoration and Transformation*

Dear John r Dee
May all the richress of the Lord's
treasure be yours!

# AVRIL VANDERMERWE

Love
Avril

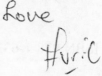 New Harbor Press

N-P New Harbor Press
www.newharborpress.com

The anecdotal illustrations in this book are the true to life experiences of the author. The names of other persons involved have been fictionalized. All other illustrations are composites of real situations, and any resemblance to people living or dead is coincidental. The story of Colton Harris Moore is in the public domain.

Unless otherwise indicated, all Scripture quotations are taken from the NIV Study Bible, 10th Anniversary Edition © 1995 by Zondervan. Scripture quotations are given in italics. Where quotations involve direct speech, quotation marks are added. All emphases are mine.

ISBN 978-1-63357-081-8

Other Books by Avril VanderMerwe

Adults

*Bible Stories for Big People: Volume 1, Old Testament*

Children

*How Cheetah Got His Tears*

Fraught with penetrating practicality, FROM TRASH TO TREASURE offers reality-based perspective, and Biblically-centered hope in a delightful package that includes real-life accounts illustrating the power of transforming grace in and through the challenges of life. Avril's inviting writing style welcomes the reader into a fresh experience with the Lord Who will redeem and repurpose life's junk into beautiful jewels. Avril uses picturesque language with the skills of a gifted writer to bring the reader into a place of fresh hope with a renewed sense of divine destiny.

Dr. Bryan K Johnson
President, Cross-National Partnerships; Former Dean, Seattle Bible College

FROM TRASH TO TREASURE is filled with practical real life analogies to bring home the message with a healthy feel and inspirational blessing. Its words are life-changing as it searches out the 'hidden trash' in our lives, either forgotten or unaware, that stymies us, replacing it with re-claimed freedom, through suggested persuasive powerful prayers. It is a thought-provoking read, motivating action for free abundant living. It stimulates movement in our lives, totally 'dumping the trash' once and for all; seeking wholeness from brokenness, redeeming and restoring true freedom in Christ.

Shirl DeBay, Ph.D, Psychologist

FROM TRASH TO TREASURE is an ideal book for any who have ever struggled with self- worth or have questioned God's love. This book is also ideal for those who help others discover God's truth about who they are and whose they are. Avril VanderMerwe takes the reader on a journey of discovering God's redemptive plan, revealing God's power through Christ to transform our personal trash. Sharing from her own life experiences as well as from examples in Scripture, Avril addresses such issues as identity, fear, control, trust, and forgiveness. At the end of each chapter, she challenges the reader to examine his or her own life, giving an invitation to pray, acknowledge need, repent, and surrender to God's will. Having served in ministry for over forty years, I highly recommend this book for personal spiritual growth and as a guide for professional, Biblical counseling.

Dr. Kathleen M. Troll

Dean, Seattle Bible College; Director, By His Grace Ministries & Word of Hope Retreats

Avril VanderMerwe, from South Africa, shows in this passionate book how the trash in our lives, whether it be mental, physical, emotional, spiritual or circumstantial, can be transformed by Jesus. She gives many examples and descriptions that paint a beautiful picture with words. She has experienced what she writes about, and the love of God shines through her with passion to share how much God loves us. It is a great book for individuals or a Bible study group, with great scriptures, and each chapter ends with a provocative question and prayer. Avril truly shows us how to give our trash to Jesus to "make something beautiful out of our lives".

Patricia Olson

Retired Principal and Daycare Director; Fulbright Alumnus

To Africa's treasure, Africa's future,
Africa's children:
Treasured by God

# ACKNOWLEDGEMENTS

Thank you to my Dad, Rev. Dr. Bill van der Merwe, who first suggested that I transcribe my messages on the "Trash to Treasure" theme, into a book. Without his input, this book would never have been written! Thank you to both him and my Mom, Lorraine van der Merwe, for their unstinting encouragement and affirmation.

My "Creatives" group of fellow writers and artists is a lifeline throughout all my writing endeavors. Thank you for your companionship and encouragement on this journey and in this calling, Deena Wilson, Diane Fink, Libby Goehner, Karen Anderson, and Theresa Leake.

Thank you to my dear friend Glenda Salmon, who has never failed to be an encouragement, including of my writing efforts! Time and distance have not dulled our valued friendship!

Thank you to all those who read the manuscript and provided feedback and endorsements:

Dr. Bryan Johnson, Anna Johnson, Dr. Shirl DeBay, Dr. Kathy Troll, Pat Olson.

Most of all, thank You to the "lover of my soul", Redeemer, Restorer, Healer... our Lord and Savior, Jesus Christ, for all His overwhelming love and mercies.

# CONTENTS

*"I want you to promise the Lord that, from tonight, you will not think back, look back, or act back!" - Smith Wigglesworth*

# CHAPTER 1
# GOT TRASH?

*T*oys! What child doesn't love new toys! In 2013 alone, the toy industry in America generated $22.09 billion in sales[1]. The homes of many American children today overflow with a glorious glut of colorful choices for their playing pleasure.

In stark contrast, thousands of children in regions of wretched poverty in parts of Africa, live a comparatively colorless existence. Most have never seen a store-bought toy. Instead, families are consumed by the hand-to-mouth struggle of scraping together just one meal a day for each family or community member. The more fortunate manage to send their children to school for a highly-prized education. Even then, commodities such as shoes and school supplies are a rarity.

As long as children are fed, sheltered, schooled and healthy, and as long as they have at least one robust parent to care for them, the family is considered prosperous indeed. Thriving children help with the work of the family, and still have the energy, curiosity and

---

[1]     www.statista.com

ingenuity to devise ways of occupying themselves without mass-manufactured playthings. Their playground is the world outside the door of a hut or shack, their play equipment whatever they discover in that environment.

Other people's trash becomes their treasure. From pieces of wire, wood, sticks, washers, rubber and tin, they fashion a variety of toy cars, trucks, motorcycles, aircraft and bicycles. Dolls are made from scraps of rags, discarded beads and bits of wool. Children spend happy hours devising games and friendly competition with these remarkable toys made out of... trash!

Yet it does not stop there. Both children and adults craft musical instruments too, from bottles, bottle tops, cans, wire, wood, gourds, seed pods, animal skin, string, sticks, oil cans... and just about any other discarded material that can be scrounged from the immediate environment. These musical instruments produce the vibrant sounds and rhythms so uniquely African. Together children, teenagers and adults create a symphony of sound captivating, haunting and beautiful – while listeners dance their joy and enjoyment to the irresistible rhythms. I have stood in a marketplace listening to a band play the most compelling music I have ever heard, on these instruments made of... trash!

In the words of television advertising, "But wait, there's more!" Men and women also produce unique and innovative crafts and art work from found materials. Many of us are familiar with the basket weaving and bead work of African and other cultures. These baskets are woven not only from natural materials, but also out of the discarded wire from old analog telephones and computer cables, making the most colorful baskets of all: the Zulu wire baskets of South Africa.

Ingenuity does not stop there. Even used teabags do not go to waste. Women collect these, and dry them out under the African sun, before emptying the tea leaves, then painstakingly ironing each bag. They mix paints in the hues of Africa, and carefully sew the ironed teabags together into canvases of various sizes, depending on the final product. With painstaking care, they paint striking designs onto these teabag canvases, transforming them into wall hangings, picture and mirror frames, bed covers, greeting cards, coasters, bookmarks... All from used teabags originally destined for the... trash!

What may be little more than throwaway junk to you and me, in the right hands is transformed into something useful, something lovely, something that produces a beautiful sound. Nothing is wasted. Tourists come from all over the world to buy these creative treasures – the toys, instruments and artwork of Africa made from... trash.

Have you taken your trash out today? Is there an argument in your household, as to whose turn, or whose job it is to take out the trash? Is this a chore put off to the last minute while you manage your life around the filling trash can until it is almost overflowing, before it is dragged out, perhaps just in time for trash collection day? What ultimately happens to that trash then? How often do you look at your trash and think, "We really should keep all of this stuff, because it could be turned into something useful and beautiful!" Imagine decorating your home with your own reclaimed trash! No doubt there are a few passionately committed individuals who do something close to this, but they are the rare exceptions.

In the western world, recycling and "going green" have become the twenty-first century's new religion. It helps that we have somewhere to dispose of our trash, someone else to collect it, someone else to recycle it. Beyond that, we do not give it much thought. Yet not all of our trash is recyclable. Thousands of tons of our throw-away, non-recyclable junk ends up in landfills all over this planet. By contrast, poverty-stricken rural African people have nowhere to dump their trash, no one to collect it, nowhere to send it for recycling. Either it lies around, cluttering and stinking up the environment, or someone takes the initiative in transforming it into something useful, good and beautiful.

All of this refers to material trash. Yet the detritus of daily living is not the only waste we accumulate and discard and pile up in landfills. What about the garbage of our personal lives – the "trash" we collect in our thoughts and experiences and emotions?

The trash from times when others have wronged us, hurt us, betrayed us, abandoned us, slandered us.

The trash from the times when we have messed up – the mistakes and wrong decisions we've made, the things we have said and done that we shouldn't have, the things we have failed to do or say.

The trash from circumstances beyond our control that have swept through our lives like a tsunami, leaving only rubble and loss in their wake.

The trash of the broken pieces of our relationships.

The trash of the same old same old destructive cycles endlessly repeated in our lives.

What do we do with the experiences in life that have left us with so much personal junk?

Where do we go with the violation and alienation and bereavement and regret, with the wounded, hollowed out, lost, broken and shameful feelings we are left with? The experiences that seem to shout "Failure!" over our lives...

An old bumper sticker expresses this truth: "I know I'm somebody 'cause God don't make no junk!"[2] Nevertheless, in one way or another, and to some degree or other, we all manage to **accumulate** a grievous amount of personal "junk" in our lives.

Deep in our hearts, we tend to identify ourselves on the basis of our trash. Somewhere inside, an insidious whisper calls out the labels of our trash-induced identity: failure, insignificant, unattractive, unimportant, incompetent, unworthy, untrustworthy, worthless, not good enough...

A few years ago I took a mid-week day trip with my family, to a local ski resort. Since we all grew up in South Africa, none of us has learned to ski, but we enjoy the snow. It was the beginning of winter and bitterly cold. The ski lifts were not yet open for the season, and not many people were about. We ended up taking refuge in the ski lodge for warmth. The only other people inside, were the members of a young family – Mom, Dad, preschooler and toddler.

Dad had a camera and was taking one picture after another, of his two-year-old son. His little girl, aged about four, kept calling, "Look at me, Daddy! Look what I can do! Take a picture of me, Daddy!" But her Dad continued to ignore her in favor of her little brother. Her Mom's attention too, was focused on the little boy.

---

[2]     Ethel Waters

My heart ached as I watched this scene play out, and I wondered what hurtful pieces of "trash" this little girl collected that day – and how those impacted her sense of self, her sense of worth.

We all have experiences in life that end up in our personal "landfill" – experiences that sully our sense of personal identity. Yet in spite of all the excess that the modern, civilized world has to offer, we find that it provides nowhere for us to go with the collected detritus of our personal lives. There is no trash collection service, no recycling program for this kind of trash - and so we carry it around with us, an endless weight from which we find no relief. Perhaps we get to unpack it from time to time, to submit it cautiously to the view of a counselor or a friend. But when that discussion is over, we pack it all up again, and carry it back home where it continues to trip us up or weigh us down.

Somehow most of us manage our lives around it, stuffing it into some dark closet of our hearts, where we try to ignore it as much as possible. We hope that nobody else sees it – after all we do not want to stink up the landscape of our lives with it or clutter our relationships with it, do we? So we skirt around it, and live past it:

perhaps by withdrawing from the world to prevent any further access to our hearts;

perhaps by living our lives in fierce independence, our defenses firmly in place;

perhaps by putting on our game face, throwing our energies into one activity after another;

perhaps by becoming fiercely territorial and competitive, keeping our insecurities well masked;

perhaps by becoming chronically self-effacing;

perhaps by exercising self-destructive control over one or two areas of our lives, resulting in eating disorders or obsessive behaviors or fraught relationships.

perhaps by becoming critical and judgmental and rude and dismissive towards others – wounding them before they can wound us.

From time to time an indefinable longing may prompt us to peer out from behind the barriers we have erected, yearning for something better, for a day when we can live free of the load we carry. Then fear or hopelessness or cynicism drives us back behind our self-erected barricades, and we continue with life as best we can.

After all, our coping strategies work up to a point. We get on with living our lives, building our careers, enjoying a measure of success, and all seems well, until… Until those times when the door of that dark closet in our hearts bursts open, spilling its unwanted junk across the threshold of our lives once again, compelling us to wade yet again through remembered pain and blighted hope and irretrievable regret – the bitter stink of it all overwhelming our senses.

Perhaps it bursts open through our dreams, or perhaps an encounter or incident or conversation springs the latch on the door we have tried to keep so firmly shut. Each time we are faced yet again with the question of what to do with all the overflowing trash of life. Again, for a fleeting moment, a longing stirs for some safe place to take this junk. A place where it can be decontaminated, its toxins neutralized, its weight lightened, our lives made whole again. But there has never been such a place before, so why should it be any different this time?

So wading through the garbage, we gather the courage and determination to sweep it all up, and for the umpteenth time, stuff it back into that dark closet, and with a supreme effort, wrestle the door shut. And we go on with our lives – until the next time that door inevitably bursts open, spilling its trash once more.

But...

But what if...?

What if that trash, given into the right hands, need not keep contaminating our lives, need not be simply discarded or merely recycled, but instead transformed! Transformed into something useful, something lovely, something that produces a beautiful sound arising from our lives?

Let's get personal. How would **you** respond if someone was willing to step up to that dark closet with you, so that you do not have to empty it alone? What if that someone made you an offer you cannot refuse: "Oh please, give all this trash to Me. Put it in My hands – and watch and see into what beauty I will transform it. And then I'll help you take the door off of this dark closet. We'll disinfect it of all its past, and paint it out in new colors. We'll leave the door standing wide open, and fill it with light and life and love and song and fragrance – and it will never be dark again!"

This is exactly what redemption is! That is exactly what Jesus came to do! So often we think of God's redemption only in terms of His paying the price, on our behalf, for our sin. And it is this – but it is also so very much more! He says it so clearly in Isaiah 61 – words that Jesus himself read out loud as a description of what He came to do: *"... He has sent Me to **bind up the brokenhearted**, to **proclaim freedom** for the captives and **release from darkness** for the prisoners...*

*to comfort all who mourn, and provide for those who grieve… to bestow on them a crown of beauty instead of ashes, the oil of gladness instead of mourning, and a garment of praise instead of a spirit of despair. They will be called oaks of righteousness, a planting of the Lord for the display of His splendor. ".*

Not recycled trash, but trash **transformed** into treasure! In ancient times, when someone was in deep pain, distress, sorrow, regret or shame, they would throw burnt ashes all over their heads. This is what Job did after experiencing the loss of his family, possessions and health. But Jesus says that He has come to transform those ashes of pain and shame and regret heaped on our heads – not discard them, or replace them, or recycle them, but **transform** them – so that our lives become crowned instead with radiant glory, and beauty, and victory, and joy!

If material trash, in the hands of African people, can be transformed into that which is so good and beautiful and unique that visitors come from all over the world to buy it, can you just imagine what our personal "trash" could become in the hands of the Creator of all the universe?

The Bible is filled with promises of the Lord's ongoing work of redemption in our lives:

*Psalm 71:20 - Though you have made me see troubles, many and bitter, you will **restore** my life again; from the depths of the earth you will again bring me up.*

What troubles have you seen and experienced that have left you wounded and wary and bitter? God promises to restore new life in the place of old woundedness!

*Zechariah 9:12 - Return to your fortress, O **prisoners of hope**; even now I announce that I will **restore** twice as much to you.*

What has caused you to become a prisoner of past pain and despair and hopelessness? He will set you free to become instead captivated by joyful hope – and then He will fulfill that hope by restoring a double portion of all that seemed so lost to you!

*1 Peter 5:10 - And the God of all grace, who called you to his eternal glory in Christ, after you have suffered a little while, will himself **restore** you and make you strong, firm and steadfast.*

No longer victims of the past but victors in the present and conquerors in the future!

The experiences and circumstances in life that seem the trashiest of all, are the very things that will shine with the radiance of God's beauty and splendor when given into His hands.

Are you tired of carrying trash around, tired of trying to live past or around the trash of your personal life? The trash of loss, of broken relationships, of mistakes made, of injustices suffered... Whether it is trash from thirty years ago, or trash from last year, or trash from last week or yesterday or even today, Jesus invites you to open up the dark closet in your heart, and allow Him to take the trash hidden there in His hands. Then watch what happens as in those hands, it is transformed into...

something useful...

something lovely...

something that produces a beautiful sound and a sweet fragrance from your life...

something radiant with the glory of God...
For the display of His splendor.

*You will be a crown of splendor in the Lord's hand, a royal diadem in the hand of your God (Isaiah 62:3).*

---

### What About You?

1. Identify what "trash" you been carrying around, emotionally, mentally, relationally, spiritually — whether brought on by other people or circumstances, or caused by your own words, actions, choices, or decisions.

2. If you are willing to open your heart to God's redemptive power working to transform your "trash" into His "treasure", pray the following prayer:
   "Jesus thank You that you are my Redeemer, and that You redeem all things. I open my heart to You now, to take the trash I have accumulated there, and to transform it by Your power. I put all my trust in You, to accomplish this in Your own wonderful way, as I commit myself to Your loving, all-powerful care."

# CHAPTER 2
# MASTER RESTORER

Every year I attend the classic car show held in Edmonds, the lovely town on the Puget Sound, where I live. I enjoy classic car shows immensely, and this one does not disappoint. The cars on display are meticulously cared for: the outside paint jobs are not only executed to perfection, but also lovingly shined to a high gloss with careful polishing; the interiors of the cars are works of art in their leather upholstery and gleaming dashboard instruments; the engines purr with well-oiled precision. As someone who originally hails from South Africa, I particularly get a kick out of seeing some of the restored British cars that are rarely seen in the United States, like the Morris 1000 and the MG Sports.

However, what fascinates me most at these car shows is seeing the pictures of the cars in their state prior to restoration. They are hardly recognizable as the same cars! Dirt, rust and general decrepitude prevail; many are stripped down to little more than their chassis, with other random parts lying discarded around them. Who knows what long roads and weary miles each car traveled, causing it to be reduced to little more than discarded wreckage, fit for only, well… the trash!

Yet there came a day in the "life" of each car, when someone came along and saw in that grimy heap of junk, the beauty to which it could one day be restored. It takes a classic car enthusiast, first of all, to see the potential beauty in all those rusted parts; it also takes an enthusiast to pay good money in order to take that heap of junk home with him or her, and to then pour time, trouble, patience and further expense into the work of restoring and transforming a pile of broken and discarded car parts into something that becomes the envy of car show attendees!

In fact, at the most recent Classic Car Show I attended, I came across the following story on display beside one of the restored cars: "I'm a 1960 Nash Metropolitan. I used to live in a field in Illinois where they kept taking parts off me to put on other cars. I was an unloved, rusting orphan. So I roamed the country coast to coast reacquiring my parts. I finally ran into Jackie and Pete and slowly but surely we're getting the rest of me back together." To this, the owners had added the following Shakespearian quote: "And, though she be but little, she is fierce"![3]

Have you ever felt as if all that is left of your life is dirt and rust and random discarded parts? Have you ever felt like a broken down, "unloved, rusting orphan"? There is good news for you!

Our Redeemer and Restorer is an enthusiast! He is enthusiastic about you and I …*He rescued me because He **delighted** in me (Psalm 18:19b)*.

He sees us with eyes that look beyond the junk to the potential beauty of our lives. He has already paid the highest price in order to

[3]    A Midsummer Night's Dream, Act 3, Scene 2

adopt us as His own, and then He pours Himself into us to produce in us the beauty He always knew was possible!

I have never seen anyone at a classic car show – owner or spectator – agonizing over the pictures of the cars prior to restoration, and mourning their past trashed state. No! It is their **restored** condition that is the focus of attention. The only effect those old photographs have, is to inspire wonder in everybody, at the transformation that has taken place!

We need never keep agonizing over the wreckage of the past; we need never continue being held captive to the trash of the past. Instead we rejoice over the restoration that is our present and future reality. *Therefore, if anyone is in Christ, he is a **new** creation; **the old has gone,** the **new** has come!* The apostle Paul writes these words in 2 Corinthians 5:17, and later goes on to tell another group of believers in Philippians, *I press on to take hold of that for which Christ Jesus took hold of me… **Forgetting what is behind** and straining toward what is ahead, I press on… (Philippians 3:12-14).*

Sometimes it seems that we have become so accustomed to living out of a place of "wreckage", that we have made it our identity. We are reluctant to embrace our new identity as "new creations" because living out of a place of restoration feels unfamiliar – and perhaps frightening. We become afraid of "driving around" in our newly restored state, instead continuing to hide out in the junkyard of the past.

However, we need not give ourselves over to rust among those ruins! Instead we should turn our focus on the Master Restorer who has bought and brought about our transformation, and continue to trust that He will empower our new identity in Him. It is then that the most broken and most shameful places in our lives become the very places that most shine with the wonder of the glory of God.

I knew someone once, a family friend, who owned a vintage car – a 1946 Triumph Roadster. He was a perfectionist, and had meticulously restored the car to what you and I might see as mint condition – in fact, my sister and brother-in-law used it in their wedding procession. Yet our friend never stopped working on that car throughout his whole life. He knew that no matter how good it looked outwardly, there were still things that needed the touch of the restorer's hand – a small part here, an adjustment there, a little more polish and a touch more elbow grease.

God's work of restoration is an ongoing process that continues throughout our whole lives. Yet long before that work is complete, we begin to gleam with the evidence of the Restorer's touch for all to see. Turning our faces to Him and making Him the focus of our attention causes our lives to reflect His radiance as He transforms us: *And we, who with unveiled faces all **reflect the Lord's glory**, are being **transformed** into His likeness **with ever-increasing glory**, which comes from the Lord, who is the Spirit (2 Corinthians 3:18).*

Our faces can only reflect whatever they are turned towards. If we are constantly focused on pain and woundedness and regret and loss and bitterness, that is what our lives will reflect. If instead we are constantly focused on the love and power and radiance and grace and faithfulness of Jesus, made so abundantly available to us, then our lives will reflect all that He is.

In addition, His peace permeates our beings when we make Him our focus: *You will keep Him in perfect peace whose mind is stayed* (fixed, riveted) *on You, because he trusts in You (Isaiah 26:3 NKJV).*

Conversely, when we keep mulling over all that is wrong with our lives, we will be constantly plagued by agitation and anxiety.

One of the things I love, is the sound of revving engines as restored classic cars parade in and out of town to and from the car show. There is something triumphant about that sound! Seeing and hearing scores of these cars parading down the road together is testament to a work of restoration that has overcome the challenges of their ruin, enabling them to become fully functional and useful once again.

*But thanks be to God, who always leads us in **triumphal** procession in Christ... (2 Corinthians 2:14).*

A "triumphal procession" refers to the Roman military custom of marching in triumphant formation through the city of Rome after successfully defeating their enemies. Very often these soldiers would force their defeated captives to parade along behind them, as objects of public shame and ridicule before the cheering, jeering citizens.

We need not be held captive to the ruin of the past. Instead, our past is taken captive by our Redeemer and Victor, Jesus Christ, and we get to parade His victory in our lives! Ephesians 4:8 tells us, *When He ascended on high, He led captives in His train and gave gifts to men.* In the words of the New King James translation, *He took captivity captive.*

Jesus Christ now "holds captive" the past that once held us in captivity. No more need we be paralyzed and incapacitated by what seemed broken down in our lives. Instead our Master Restorer sets us back on the road, displaying His handiwork in His victory parade, having made us fit for His use once again. You and I too, can become a restored "Triumph" with a capital "T"!

Something else I enjoy about restored vintage cars, is the smell of the re-covered leather seats. Restored cars carry the aroma of their restoration with them! Verse 14 in 2 Corinthians goes on to say *... and through us spreads everywhere the **fragrance** of the knowledge of Him.*

God's work of transformation in us becomes so evident that through us the very atmosphere is permeated with the sweet aroma of Jesus Christ:

Notice that this "fragrance" is derived from "knowing" Christ. Not just knowing about Him intellectually, but knowing Him in a personally relational and experiential way. The more we know Him this way, the more we are transformed into His work of restoration, and the more He is on display in our lives. Transformation is not about God waving a magic wand and "fixing" everything that is wrong. Rather, transformation is relational and takes place as a result of ever-deepening relationship with God through Jesus Christ, in the power of the Holy Spirit.

No matter what long, rocky roads or weary miles we have traveled that seem to have rattled us into a state of wreckage, His power restores and transforms that wreckage – and never stops transforming it for all the rest of our lives! A small part here, an adjustment there, a little more polish and touch of Divine elbow grease...

Enslaving ourselves to the past by making it the dominating focus of our attention, is one of the things that hinders us from living the abundant life that Jesus promises us in the present. Not only does He hold captive our past captivity to wreckage, but He transforms it into something that fills the atmosphere with the revelation of who He is. We will not find the resolution to our life's "trash" anywhere else.

JESUS is Almighty Redeemer!

JESUS is Master Restorer!

JESUS is the Lion of the tribe of Judah, who breaks every chain of bondage to the past and sets us free, for once and for all! The words of one of my favorite songs as a child say:

> *For the Lion of Judah shall break every chain*
> *And give us the victory again and again![4]*

JESUS is the One who takes all the broken down junk of our lives and from it produces...

something useful...

something beautiful...

something producing a victorious sound and a pleasing aroma...

You are His prize-winning classic, a loving work of restoration undertaken by the greatest Creator, Redeemer and Restorer of all!

---

[4]     Lyrics by H. Q. Wilson

## What About You?

1. Identify those areas or seasons of your life that seem to have lain in ruins, and that you have continued to mourn over.

2. If you long to experience the touch of the Master Restorer's hand in those areas, pray this prayer: "Lord I don't know what to do with all the wreckage of the past. I don't know how to fit the pieces back together again. But thank You that You are able to accomplish what I am not — even far beyond anything I could ask or imagine. I hand these broken pieces over to You right now, and ask that You begin to work Your restoration power in all the wrecked places of my life."

# CHAPTER 3
# WASTED YEARS

For months the public in the Pacific Northwest, and later, around the country and even the world, was gripped by the news stories and unsuccessful police pursuit of "The Barefoot Bandit": Colton Harris-Moore. Escaping from a detention center in western Washington, he went on the run at only 17 years old, and over the following two years, broke into over a hundred private residences and stole several cars, boats, and airplanes.

Colton had an unstable family life, and a dysfunctional upbringing, and by the age of seven, had started living alone in the wild for stretches at a time. By the time he was twelve, he was living in a tree-house in the woods. In order to sustain himself, he would break into vacation homes to steal blankets, food and water to take with him into the forest. By the age of thirteen, he had four convictions of stolen property against him. The consequence of each conviction was either a ten-day stay in a detention center, or community service. However, in 2003 a stolen camcorder was found in his possession, and this time his sentence was three years. Since the age of seven, Colton had never been confined anywhere for very long. Three years of confinement was unthinkable. He walked out of the halfway house in April 2008, and made a run for it.

Although he caused a lot of property loss and damage, the public developed something of a fascination for Colton. His adventures and string of thefts started on Camano Island in western Washington then spread to the San Juan Islands and British Columbia, Canada, before blazing a trail through Idaho, South Dakota, Nebraska, Iowa and Illinois. Finally, on July 4, 2010, a Cessna single-engine airplane went missing from the Bloomingdale, Illinois airport, and was later found crashed on the beach of Great Abaco Island in the Bahamas.

It was the Bahamas police who finally caught up with Colton, early in the morning of July 11, 2010, at Harbour Island. After the appropriate legal procedures in first the Bahamas, then Florida, Colton was transferred back to the state of Washington, where at time of writing, he is serving his sentence at Stafford Creek Corrections Center.

However, it is not Colton's exploits that are most noteworthy. What is striking are the words of this highly intelligent young man to his public defender in the Bahamas: "I would have lived life a little differently if I had the chance to do it again."

*Wasted years, wasted years, oh how foolish*[5]... So go the words of an old song that articulates this regret. If only I had the time over, I would do things differently, react differently, choose differently... How many times have you thought or said those words? Colton Harris-Moore cannot get the time back — and neither can you or I. But Jesus promises that when we surrender our lives to Him, He redeems the wasted years of the past, and fills our present and our

[5]     Wally Fowler 1959

future so abundantly, that our past becomes "bought back", and its mess becomes a Divine work of renewal.

So often we grieve over the days, weeks, months, years, or seasons that seem to have laid waste the landscape of our lives. We mourn the time we can never get back, spending our energy on regret. If only we would place our hope in the One who makes this promise: *I will repay you for the years the locusts have eaten— the great locust and the young locust, the other locusts and the locust swarm — my great army that I sent among you (Joel 2:25).*

Have you ever seen a locust swarm? Have you ever experienced the devastation left behind by these insects? Certain areas of South Africa, like many parts of the world, are plagued by locust swarms from time to time. When the locust swarm flies into an area, the millions of insects swarming together form what looks like a dark, ominous cloud rapidly approaching. A low, threatening buzz fills the air. Once the locusts land, every bit of greenery is stripped and destroyed within minutes as they devour every green and living plant in sight. When they lift off to migrate to the next area, they leave behind them a wilderness of devastation. The life and fruitfulness of the land is laid waste. Farmers who have labored all year over their crops, see their work destroyed in one disastrous instant.

Is this a picture of your life? Have circumstances and experiences afflicted you in such a way that it feels as if they have rendered your life blighted and barren and stripped of all fruitfulness? Have you poured yourself into relationships or family or employment or church, only to have all your months and years of effort laid waste by destructive experiences or circumstances?

If so, this promise from the book of Joel is God's promise to you! It speaks of every wasted period of your life being gloriously reclaimed and transformed into a life filled with God's purpose, and restored – and greater - fruitfulness!

How God accomplishes this in each life will be specific and unique to each person. The story He is writing, and the purpose He is accomplishing is different for each individual. But one thing we can be sure of: nothing is wasted in His kingdom!

Joseph was betrayed, sold out, falsely accused and imprisoned. He spent seemingly wasted years first in slavery, then in prison. Yet God brought about his release from prison at exactly the right moment for him to step into a position of authority in the land – a position for which all his hard experiences through all those long years, had perfectly prepared him.

Moses ended up in an interminable wilderness, seeming to waste away the prime years of his life: until God called him as His agent of deliverance for an entire nation. It turned out that those forty years leading sheep around the wilderness were perfect training for leading a million people through that same wilderness to the Promised Land.

David was overlooked, dismissed, mocked, betrayed by those closest to him, hounded, his life threatened, and he spent years on the run from King Saul: All of which honed his character and his faith to make him God's chosen and most revered and beloved king to lead Israel.

Daniel was taken captive as an adolescent, to spend his whole life in service to one pagan king after another: Yet rather than giving up and bewailing his misfortunes, those years were filled with Divine purpose as through him God revealed himself to those same kings, and ultimately through Daniel's intercessions, God's people were released from their captivity.

The whole Bible is filled with one story after another, of individuals who suffered reverses that seemed to lay waste the years of their lives. Yet God so powerfully redeemed the time that seemed lost and rendered barren, that what we now know these individuals for is not their misfortunes, but the great impact and fruitfulness of their lives.

No, we cannot get our "wasted years" back. But in the above-mentioned passage, God promises to **repay** us for those years. We cannot relive the past, but we **can** live **today** – and all the "todays" that follow – as days filled with God-given purpose.

In Psalm 138:8 we read these wonderful words: *The Lord will perfect that which concerns me… (NKJV)*.

We need not stress about the "how" or strive to bring about the reclamation of the past ourselves. All we need to do is abandon ourselves in trust to the One who has given us His word on the matter – and live each day to its fullest for Him. We are not able to see the whole picture of our own lives: He is the only One who is able to see the whole sweep of our life's landscape; He is the only One who knows exactly where to place the next brushstroke; He is the only One who knows how the dark portions fit into the beauty of the whole.

Have you ever seen a large mosaic, like the mosaic walls and floors that were built during the time of the Roman Empire? If you had to walk up to a mosaic design, and press your nose against just one mosaic tile until it was the only one you could see, it would seem meaningless and pointless: a small, bland tile with no bearing on anything. But viewed in the context of the whole picture, each piece of mosaic is essential to the whole — if any small piece was missing, the picture would be spoiled and incomplete.

In the same way, each part of our lives is absolutely necessary to the next one, and to the whole design of our lives. Sometimes our view of life is so consumed by one experience, or by what looks dark and hopeless, that we are unable to see its place and purpose in the whole scope of our lives. Yet from the perspective of the One who is the Creator of the whole detailed, intricate, exquisite picture, not a single piece of it is wasted or superfluous.

No, He does not send destructive circumstances into our lives. Those come about through the sinful acts of others or ourselves. But He does redeem them and repurpose them, until we too can say with Joseph, "*You intended to harm me, but God intended it for good to accomplish what is now being done, the saving of many lives*" *(Genesis 50:20).*

### What About You?

1. Identify the seasons or years of your life that feel as if they have been left devastated.

2. Declare Joel 2:25 over these specific time periods in your life, and pray the following prayer:
   "Father, I come to you as a little child. I confess that I have no ability of my own to reclaim what feels like seasons and years laid waste in my life. And even though I don't know how You will accomplish it, I thank You that Your Word is true, and Your promises are sure. And so with the trust of a little child, I ask You to indeed reclaim and restore all the "years that the locust has eaten" in my life, and to put on display Your victory and Your glory in the very areas that seem to have suffered the most devastation."

# CHAPTER 4
# COME THIRSTY

*P*erhaps when you hear or read such a message, your heart is moved. Deep in a place that you have kept hidden for a long time, something begins to throb like a wound. A new thirst is awakened – thirst for... something... Hope begins to stir – hope that perhaps, after all, your "trash" could finally stop stinking up your life, and maybe, just maybe, even be transformed into something good, something beautiful.

But how?

Many years ago, in my early to middle twenties, I felt as if I was bent under a load of trash that overwhelmed my life. It was trash that felt like a mountain of splintered glass shards that stabbed my heart with every breath I took. A doctor diagnosed me with "clinical reactive depression" from years of stress and trauma, and prescribed anti-depressants.

But I knew I needed an answer that could not be found in a doctor's office or a pharmacy. I read these words from Ecclesiastes

3:11: *He has made everything beautiful in its time. He has also set eternity in the hearts of men...*

Eternity in the hearts of men... If the trash in my life was to be transformed into something beautiful, and if God has set eternity in my heart, then the only way for such transformation to be accomplished was for me to turn my brokenness over to the One who is Himself eternal and open my heart deeply and completely to Him.

Every day, immediately upon arriving home from work, I would close the door of my apartment behind me, fling my bags into a corner, and fall on my face in the presence of the Eternal One. I came to Him because I was hurting, and there was no other place to go where my hurts could be healed. But before very long, my prayers began to change. Instead of asking for my hurts to be healed, I began to open my heart to all that God is, and to ask Him for more and more of... Him. Now instead of hurting, I was thirsty – for Him. As I immersed myself in Him, without my even realizing it, the heap of trash in my life grew smaller, the wounds closed, a new lightness energized my steps, a new zest for life fueled me. Before long, the trash of my life was transformed into a passion for God and His Word, and a compassion for the broken and hurting around me. I was no longer consumed with pain – I was consumed by Jesus. And the trash was gone.

He did more than transform my trash: He completely satisfied a deep, inexpressible thirst. He filled the eternity that He had set in my heart, with Himself.

This reminds me of a true story of something that happened more than two thousand years ago:

In a day before cars, trains and airplanes had been invented, thirteen men were travelling together from Judea to Galilee – a distance of about 70 miles, taking the direct route. Nevertheless, most people preferred to double the distance of their journey by taking the long way around, rather than travel through the region inhabited by those despised half-breeds, the Samaritans.

However, these thirteen men were different. They made no effort to avoid that area. Instead they intentionally struck out along the direct route straight through Samaria. On each side of the road stood fields of carefully cultivated wheat, barley, grapes and olive trees. Yet the road itself was dry and dusty under a blistering sun, and walking the distance was tiring and thirsty business. Much in need of rest and refreshment, the men stopped at a town in Samaria called Sychar. One of the men sat and rested at Jacob's Well just outside the town, while the others went into the marketplace to purchase food for them all. So it was that Jesus sat alone at the well, awaiting the return of His disciples with the supplies.

It was while He waited that the lone figure of a woman appeared, walking from the town towards the well to draw water. A common enough event in ancient Palestine, one might think. However, there were at least two uncommon elements in this seemingly everyday scene. The first was that this woman did not come to draw water in the cool of the morning, as was the custom, but instead came in the middle of the day. Secondly, she came alone, instead of in the company of other women. It seems she had reason to avoid the company of decent women - or rather, they had reason to avoid her.

Seeing the man sitting at the well, her expectation was that He would move away once she drew nearer. Not only because it would not be seemly for a man alone to be seen in close proximity to a woman on her own, but also because she could see that He was a Jew, who would consider a Samaritan "unclean". Trash. To a Jewish man she was a "dog woman".

She was a little taken aback, therefore, to notice that far from moving away, He seemed to be watching her, unmoving, as she approached. Nevertheless, she did not falter. She well understood the desires of men, and perhaps she thought that here was yet another man who wanted whatever she had to offer.

Indeed, it seems He did want something from her, because as she reached the well where He sat, He asked, "Will you give me a drink of water?"

There was no mistaking the irony in her voice as she retorted, "Are you, a Jew, asking me, a Samaritan, for a drink of water?"

His answer was far from what she expected. "If you knew who it is who asks you for water," He said, "You would instead have asked Him for water, and He would have given you living water."

Perhaps the heat had made this man delusional. He was not making any sense at all! "You do not even have anything to draw water with," she shot back at Him, "How would you possibly get this so-called 'living water'!"

Jesus answered her, "Everyone who drinks the water from this well, will experience thirst again, but whoever drinks the water I give will never be thirsty again. In fact, the water I give will become like a never-ending spring of water within, water that is eternally life-giving."

Far from demanding something of her, it seemed that this man was making her an offer she couldn't refuse! The woman imagined that if she had some of this everlasting water, she would not have to keep returning to the well day after day, repeatedly running the risk of exposing her shame to the ridicule of her neighbors.

"Sir!" she exclaimed, "Please give me some of this water, so that I will not have to keep returning to this well!"

It was then that the conversation took another seemingly bizarre twist. For in response to her request for the water Jesus offered, He said, "Go get your husband and come back here."

Hanging her head in shame, the woman mumbled, "I have no husband."

Jesus responded, "You said that right! The truth is, you've had five husbands, and you're not even married to the man you're living with now!"

How did a conversation about water suddenly turn into one about this woman's personal shame? In fact, Jesus had not really changed the subject at all. He was simply highlighting what the conversation had really been about all along: A conversation about this woman's deep, inner thirst - a gnawing, insatiable thirst that she had tried, all her life, to fill with serial relationships. Yet as one relationship after another failed, no matter how many men and how many relationships she had, nothing and nobody truly seemed to satisfy her deep-down longing.

This was a woman who knew her "religion". In fact, she tried to engage Jesus in an argument over the differences between what the Jews and Samaritans believed. But rather than religion based on head knowledge and tradition, Jesus offered her instead a living encounter with Himself. He saw her desperate, inner thirst, and immediately offered what she really needed: the living water of the bottomless love of God, revealed to her in Himself, Jesus Christ. He already knew all there was to know about her. He confronted the "trash" of her life unflinchingly. Yet far from condemning her, He offered to bring life to everything in her that was filled with the stench of brokenness and decay and blighted hope. Her deep, inner thirst was filled that day. Jesus took the "trash" of her life, and transformed it forever.

She ran back into town as fast as she could, no longer so filled with shame that she could not face her neighbors, and called excitedly to everyone within earshot, "Come, see a man who told me everything I ever did!" The "living water" the woman received immediately began to flow through her to those around her. As the result of the testimony of transformation in her life, many others came to know Jesus that day. In fact, at the request of the townsfolk, He stayed in Sychar with them for several days, ministering and teaching[6].

Are you thirsty? Are you filled with the shame of your "trash"? Have you cast around for answers that never come, or tried to fill the gnawing ache in your life with one unsatisfying pursuit after another? Maybe, like the woman of Samaria, you have tried to fill it with serial relationships that provided temporary distraction, but ultimately left you empty and dry.

Perhaps you have tried to fill it with work or study or relentless ambition, or money or more and better material possessions or travel to exotic destinations, or by constant movement and activity. But somehow you never feel truly satisfied by what you achieve or what you have or the places you have been or the things you have done.

[6]      John 4:1-42

Perhaps you have tried to fill it by pursuing pleasure: Yet when the moment of pleasure is over, your sense of desolation and emptiness washes back over you like an incoming tide.

Perhaps you try to fill it with entertainment or distraction or escapism. Movies, DVDs, video games, alcohol, drugs... But when those wear off and you have to face reality once more, your pain and loneliness holds your heart in an even more crushing grip than before.

Perhaps you have tried to fill it by latching onto one resource person or methodology or philosophy after another. But sooner or later the novelty of that person or practice palls or their flaws become evident, and you find yourself searching yet again.

Jesus offers me and you an alternative to the endless, repetitious pursuit of those things that never satisfy. He offers us Himself.

Not too many years ago, a missionary lay dying of ovarian cancer. She had been a vibrant worship leader, and during the last days of her life, she sang the words of a song that plays on my CD player even as I write this:

> *Will You come and fill me*
> *Will You overwhelm me*
> *Come fill me up with Your amazing love...*[7]

Instead of being overwhelmed by her illness and weakness and the circumstances she found herself in, she was overwhelmed by all that God is. What about us? Instead of being overwhelmed by our trash, we can be overwhelmed with all that Jesus is! He not only

[7]    "Your Amazing Love" composed and sung by Nancy Ross, from the CD "In His Presence" by Phil & Cindy Porter and Dana & Nancy Ross, YWAM, Thailand.

fills us with His love, He fills us with **Himself** – and never stops filling us for all the rest of our lives. When we are continuously, completely filled with Him and His beauty, there is no space left for trash! Jesus said these words in John 7:37, 38: *"If anyone is thirsty, let him come to Me and drink. Whoever believes in Me, as the Scripture has said, streams of living water will flow from within him"*.

Are you thirsty? Come, bring all that you are to the One who offers you His living water, and be washed, and refreshed, and filled and made new. Drink of Him, and awake to a past redeemed, a life restored, a future filled with hope.

---

### What About You?

1. What have you been using to try to fill your inner sense of emptiness or "thirst?"

2. Pray this prayer: "Lord, I confess that I have been turning to _____ to try to fill my inner thirst. I hardly even know what it is I long for, but as I come to You now, I ask You to fill me with Yourself. Drench my heart with Your living water; satisfy me with Yourself; reveal to me who You are. Thank You that You know me to the innermost depths of my being. Draw me close in intimate love relationship with You, and within that intimacy, transform me by Your love and Your power."

---

# CHAPTER 5
# GET A GRIP

For twenty years I lived in the scenic city of Cape Town, South Africa. Tourists come from all over the world to revel in the beauty and rich cultural atmosphere of this jewel of the Atlantic. I love hiking, and regularly climbed the iconic Table Mountain that presides over the city.

One memorable Saturday, I set out with a friend to hike to the top of the mountain. Depending on which route one followed, the climb usually took about four or five hours, and so I carried no more than a light daypack holding a sandwich and a bottle of water. We initially set off along a route we had walked many times before – one that wound easily around and up the mountain, and provided a mesmerizing view of Table Bay.

However, partway through our hike, my friend suddenly stopped at the entrance to a small track running directly up the mountain. "I'm bored with this route," he claimed, "Let's take a route we've never done before. Why not try this one?"

I drew his attention to the sign right in front of us at the trailhead that read, "Danger! Do not proceed beyond this point unless you are an experienced climber equipped with ropes."

We were not climbers: we were hikers. And the only "ropes" we had, were the laces in our hiking boots! My friend was undeterred. "We'll be fine," he called confidently over his shoulder as he strode forward, "We're experienced hikers."

I quickly reviewed my choices: I could outright refuse to accompany him, and wait there for the hours it would take him to get back – if he ever did; I could leave him to continue alone, while I hiked back down the mountain; I could continue on our originally planned route by myself, and let him make his own choice; or... I could go with him and hope for the best.

My feet seemed to make the decision for me: I was right behind him!

At first it seemed that the warning sign had been an unnecessary caution. We certainly had hiked together over challenging and rugged terrain before, and this route seemed easily conquered by comparison. That is, until we came to the first of several crossings of a deep ravine. The drop beneath us was sheer and seemed bottomless, and the only way from one side of the ravine to the other was across a cast iron ladder precariously spanning the gap at an incline of about sixty-five degrees. The rungs of the ladder were widely spaced, and beneath yawned a heart-stopping chasm to jagged rocks far below. As if this was not challenging enough, some of the rungs were entirely rusted away, leaving extra wide gaps between steps. My friend was over six feet tall and had long legs. I am only five feet three inches! My legs were not long enough to breach the expanse from one ladder rung to the next. To make matters worse, the terrain on the other side of the ladder was not only dizzyingly steep, but consisted of layer upon layer of loose shale. A single misstep could result in a cascade of shale and helplessly flailing limbs straight down the slippery slope to the bottom of the ravine.

I turned to consider going back down the mountain rather than continuing on this foolhardy expedition: but suddenly the distance we had already come looked too precarious to negotiate downhill. My friend had already mounted the first ladder. Instinctively I realized that becoming separated from him would make me far more vulnerable to danger. Again I followed.

The terror I experienced that day has remained unmatched throughout my life so far. Monday morning newspapers frequently carried reports of people who had lost their lives on the mountain. I was convinced that we would be the subjects of the next such newspaper article. Except… there was not another soul in the world who even knew where we were that Saturday morning. We could disappear and nobody would know what had become of us.

Going back was out of the question; going forward was terrifying. It was tempting to stay frozen in place, stuck in the middle of an inadequate ladder spanning the chasm. Had I not moved, I would probably still be there, a petrified skeleton with a life unlived.

If I was to ever accomplish my goals and reach the rest of my life's potential, there was only one choice open to me that day: I had to take hold of the rungs of that ladder with all my strength, and keep moving onwards, not looking back. As it turned out, there was a succession of about six such ladders crisscrossing the ravine that lay between us and the top of the mountain. There were times when my legs could not span the gaps between missing ladder rungs, and when this happened, my friend would reach behind him, and we would clamp one another's forearms in a vise-like grip while he dragged me across the space with the ravine yawning beneath me.

I was shaking with effort and fear, but could not succumb to either as we cleared each ladder, because I had to place my every step with precision as we scrabbled up the loose shale between ravine crossings.

This experience has given me a vivid understanding of the following words written by the apostle Paul in Philippians 3:12b:

*... I press on to take hold of that for which Christ Jesus took hold of me.*

On my death-defying mountain hike, there was no going back. The only way forward was to keeping pressing on; and the only way to press on was by taking hold of either the rungs of the ladder or my friend's hand, with all my strength and energy. We finally reached the top of the mountain, triumphant and exhilarated!

Jesus does not come into our lives uninvited. But when we do invite Him in to redeem all the "trash" of our past, He takes hold of our lives both with purpose and **for** purpose. He does not do so halfheartedly, but in the fullness of His power and love. His work is supernatural and complete – He accomplishes what no human being, self-help study, support group, counselor or methodology can do. But it does not end there: with His ongoing help, we can continue to walk in the redemption, freedom, healing and deliverance He has so graciously provided. Onward and upward! And this requires that we take hold of Him and His redeeming work in our lives and His purpose for our lives, with all of our strength and energy, clinging to Him for dear life as we move forward, and putting energetic effort into our progress!

Too often I meet people who have had dramatic experiences of God's redemptive work in their lives, and yet... Somehow they seem frozen in place, not having moved on from that initial experience. They are camped out at that spot, suspended between what lies behind and what lies ahead, realizing that they can never go back, and desiring God's purposes to be fulfilled in and through their lives, but afraid of the unknown and unfamiliar lying ahead. They become spiritual skeletons petrified in place, their life's purpose and calling unlived.

Jesus Christ took hold of our lives with the intent that we should move forward in His purposes – even if there are times when our forward progress seems little more than inch by incremental inch, trembling all the way! Before long those inches will add up to a mile, then another. My Dad is a teacher of New Testament Greek, and he always tells his students: "By a mile it's a trial, but by an inch it's a cinch!"

We do not walk out our new freedom alone! The same God who redeemed all that lies behind us, is the One whose powerful hand is extended to help us move forward in His purposes. We need to take hold of Him with everything that is in us, and press on into the exhilarating and triumphant adventure of His purposes that lie before us. Onward and upward! Sure there might be some slipping and sliding along the way, and we need be careful where we set our feet – but He will never leave us, never let us go, and His intentions towards us are always good all the time! He promises that when we trust in Him, He will both direct our steps, and keep our feet from slipping:

*Trust in the Lord with all your heart and lean not on your own understanding; in all your ways acknowledge him, and he will make your paths straight (Proverbs 3:5, 6).*

*He will not let your foot slip – he who watches over you will not slumber (Psalm 121:3).*

He also promises that we will not become statistics, but rather conquering heroes through Him:

*No, in all these things we are more than conquerors through him who loved us. For I am convinced that neither death nor life, neither angels nor demons, neither the present nor the future, nor any powers, neither height nor depth, nor anything else in all creation, will be able to separate us from the love of God that is in Christ Jesus our Lord (Romans 8:37-39).*

Take hold with all your energy, of all that for which Christ Jesus laid hold of your life – hold out for His highest and best for you – and keep moving forward in His redemptive power!

In the words of Oswald Chambers, "my utmost for His highest"! His highest will carry you higher, from strength to strength and from victory to victory, even in the face of challenges along the way.

### What About You?

1. Have you been "stuck" emotionally, mentally, spiritually, or in your relationship with God, perhaps out of fear, perhaps out of passivity?

2. Whatever the reason, pray this prayer: "Lord, thank You that You did not take hold of my life for nothing. Thank You that You took hold of my life on purpose, for purpose. I long for Your perfect purposes to be fulfilled in and through my life. I commit myself, this day, to in turn take hold of You with all my heart, mind and strength, and follow You wherever and however You may lead me, in confidence that You will never let go of me, and will never let me fall."

# CHAPTER 6
# EYES FRONT!

*I*n January 2000, when I went to the travel agent's office to book my flight out of South Africa to America, I neglected to take my passport with me. However, since I had recently returned from another trip that I had booked through the same travel agent, she simply waved her hand and said, "Oh don't worry, I remember seeing your passport the last time." And she issued me a ticket to fly.

Little did she know that inwardly I was panicking. Where was my passport? I had no recollection at all as to where I had put it for safekeeping. Not wanting to alarm the travel agent, I hid my anxiety until, airplane ticket in hand, I leapt into my car and made a mad dash for home to begin the search.

I looked in all the usual places, in all the unusual places, and finally turned my home upside down and inside out (figuratively speaking, of course!). No passport. There seemed to be only one other possibility – perhaps in the stress of sorting, packing and moving, I had accidentally thrown it in the trash. With renewed hope, I began to dig through all the waste containers in the house. Still no passport.

It was time to take things to a level I had hoped to avoid. I lived outside the suburbs in a semi-rural area of small farms comprised of several acres each. Our properties had no trash collection service. Instead, we deposited our trash in a small dumpster shared by the three homes occupying the land. My sister and cousin were with me, and the three of us undertook the distasteful task of scratching through all the trash in the dumpster. There was no way of distinguishing my trash bags from those of my neighbors, so we had to search through them all. However, my passport was nowhere to be found.

The trash in this dumpster was collected once every two weeks, and taken to a large communal dumpster in the suburbs, which in turn was periodically emptied by the local trash removal company and transported to the landfill. We reached the unavoidable conclusion that my passport lay somewhere amongst the decomposing trash in this communal dumpster. There was only one thing to do: we crammed into the car, drove to the communal dumpster, and set ourselves to search through it. The task had by then moved from distasteful to disgusting.

It was the middle of summer. The trash had been baking under the South African sun for several weeks. Maggots and flies crawled everywhere. Bags had broken open and were oozing their vile contents in every direction. The stench of decay assaulted our nostrils. The dumpster was deep, long and wide. The only way to search through it was by climbing right into its mess. Almost gagging on the stink, we methodically combed through the rotting trash.

My passport was not there.

It seemed that all options were exhausted. Dejected, I made my way home, full of inner misgivings. The thought of leaving South Africa was breaking my heart, and I began to consider whether the missing passport was a sign that I should remain after all. My sister, cousin and I returned to my home, where half-filled packing boxes littered the rooms: boxes that were being packed in preparation for the future.

"Have you looked in the boxes for your passport?" It was my sister who asked the question.

"No," I replied, "It's a waste of time – there's no reason why I would have packed it away in a box!"

However, I decided to take a look anyway, just in case. And there it was! The passport that had been issued to me just six months previously, packed on top of my old, cancelled passport, which I had kept as a souvenir of my trip to Scotland several years earlier. Here I had been digging through all the stinking trash of the past, when instead the answer lay in focusing my attention on that which contained the future.

What a life lesson! While Jesus redeems the brokenness of our past, there is one kind of "trash" He simply casts away – and that is the "trash" of our sin. The Bible tells us that when we receive His forgiveness and salvation, He casts our sins away, removing them far from us, and never holding them against us again:

*He does not treat us as our sins deserve or repay us according to*
*our iniquities. For as high as the heavens are above the earth,*

*so great is his love for those who fear him; as far as the east is from the west, so far has he removed our transgressions from us (Psalm 103:10-12).*

Why then, do we go looking for the trash of our past, digging through it again and again, sloshing around in the stink of it all, and getting our spirits splattered with its muck all over again? In the previous chapter we considered those who are frozen in place – moving neither backwards nor forwards. I have also met many people whom God has wonderfully redeemed, yet who are perpetually trapped in the dumpster of their past "trash" because they keep returning to it by an act of their own will! Their lives are filled with depression and regret as they rob themselves of the present, and poison their perception of their future, because they keep returning to the morbidly obsessive misery of their past!

My use of the word "morbid" is deliberate. Morbidity has to do with death and decay. The Bible tells us that when we come to Christ through faith, our old nature is put to death. But when we insist on repeatedly returning to what is dead and discarded, the stench of death begins to permeate our spirits that are intended to be filled with the abundant life of Christ. Do you know what "abundant" means? It means extravagantly more than enough. Jesus said, *"The thief does not come except to steal, and to kill, and to destroy. I am come that they may have **life**, and that they may have it more **abundantly** (John 10:10 NKJV).*

Who is the "thief"? He is Satan, enemy of our souls. He loves few things better than to keep us chained to that which is death to us. The links in that chain are the lies that he tells us to keep us tethered to our past. We need to speak the truth of Jesus' redeeming power to those lies, and see the manacles melt away!

Have you ever seen an adult African circus elephant tethered to a stake plugged into the ground? Doesn't it look as if that old elephant could simply snap that tether or pull up that stake and walk away from the indignity of circus life? Sure he could! He is tethered to a lie that is so deeply ingrained in his thinking, that it does not even occur to him to try! When he was no more than a bitty baby elephant calf, he was securely chained to a post, and no matter how much he resisted and pulled at that thing, it kept him trapped. Eventually his smart elephant memory learned that a tether meant no possibility of escape – and so he quit trying, never realizing, once he grew to full strength and stature, that he could break his chains any time!

The enemy pulls exactly the same trick on us! Instead of living out of the reality of the power and stature we have in Jesus Christ who breaks all bonds and sets us free, we continue believing an old lie of a redundant captivity! Jesus said, *"You will know the truth, and the truth will set you free" (John 8:32)*! Here is the truth: He has broken all the power and bondage of the enemy in your life, and you **are** free! You can walk away from captivity to that morbid past, into the glorious future that God has set before you! Don't go blaming Jesus if you insist on returning to your old chain and stake in the ground because it holds a certain familiarity for you!

When we take another look at our passage in Philippians chapter 3, we read these words in verses 13b-14, words that were mentioned in a previous chapter: **Forgetting what is behind** *and straining toward* *what is ahead, I press on toward the goal to win the prize for which God has called me heavenward in Christ Jesus.*

We will never make progress in our Christian walk if we persist in turning back to the past that Christ died to redeem! When we keep returning to it, our feet become mired in its trash all over again. Instead we need to fix our attention and place our feet where our faith is – in the progressively unfolding purposes of God that lie before us.

Many people stumble over the phrase **"forgetting** what is behind". How can one simply forget the shame and regret of the past, they ask? However, this statement does not refer to a loss of memory, but rather it means to refrain from dwelling on it in negative and destructive ways that hinder our progress. The Apostle Paul clearly did not "forget" his past – in fact, he referred to his past on several recorded occasions, each time for the purpose of testimony to God's amazing work of redemption in his life!

When I was 21 years old, I had tendon graft surgery on my right ankle, to remedy an old sports injury involving torn ligaments. Some mistakes were made in the surgery, and I almost died from subsequent septicemia; I had ongoing infections for the following eighteen months, as well as five or six further surgeries. I was unable to walk in all that time, and the experience left me with a number of surgery scars crisscrossing my ankle like random railway tracks to nowhere.

Those scars are still visible today, and I still clearly remember the events that caused them. However, the scars do not hurt, I do not walk with a limp, and on a day-to-day basis I don't think about my ankle at all. The incident, while traumatic, is in the past, and the wounds have long-since healed. I moved on with my life, hiking, cycling and running. Over the years since, I have only occasionally told the story as a testament to God's hand of protection and healing on me at a time when the doctors pronounced me dying of infected blood poisoning.

I have not "forgotten" the experience – but neither do I live my life out of that experience. If I were to still hobble around on crutches, repeatedly ask for prayer for my ankle, and be too fearful to participate in any sort of exercise, I would be robbing myself of a life lived out of the truth that the poison is cleansed and the wound is healed!

However, so often this is exactly our approach to our redeemed past. Instead of living as if Jesus has cleansed, healed, delivered and redeemed us, and removed our sins from us, we persist in going back to dig through the dumpster of our past – thereby robbing ourselves of living fully in our redeemed present, and pressing on to a future filled with Divine destiny.

Notice the strong action words Paul uses: **"straining** toward what is ahead I **press** on..."** Once again, this involves energetic engagement in the present, toward a purpose-filled future. By contrast, if you have ever wasted time mulling gloomily over the past, you know the extent to which doing so saps your energy. You can be sure that the enemy rubs his hands together in great glee when our wallowing in the muck of the past leaves us too despondent, defeated and devitalized to actively co-operate with the Creator of the universe and Redeemer of our lives in the accomplishment of His purposes for us!

As I discovered through my own rooting around in the dumpster, flies are attracted to trash too. Satan is known, amongst other things, as "Beelzebub" – a name that means "lord of the flies". Guess what happens when we choose to wallow in the "trash" of our past? The stink of trash attracts the "lord of the flies" who seizes the opportunity to buzz around, oppressing us even more. No wonder we end up debilitated by gloom and afflicted with tormenting thoughts and feelings!

Recent developments in neuro-science confirm what the Bible has taught all along: that we become what we dwell and focus on. *For as he thinks in his heart, so is he (Proverbs 23:7, NKJV)*. Dr. Caroline Leaf, a neuroscientist and a Christian believer, demonstrates how allowing our thoughts to dwell on negativity, literally acts as a toxin to our brain cells, and to the cells throughout our bodies, causing them to become damaged and diseased. Conversely, prayer and worship, which entail focusing on God and His power, glory, and goodness, brings healing to our brains and bodies on a physical level as well as on an emotional and spiritual level[8].

The Bible instructs us to *be transformed by the renewing of your mind (Romans 12:2)* and to *take captive every thought to make it obedient to Christ (2 Corinthians 10:5)*. This includes bringing our thought-life into alignment and agreement with the Word of God. For example, "I am the redeemed of the Lord. He calls me by name and I am His. His work of redemption in my life is both a completed and an ongoing work – He does not overlook any part of it! The power of His Word is alive and active in my life. All His promises are true, and He is faithful in keeping them. Nothing can snatch me out of His hand, and He does all things well in my life.

---

8        drleaf.com

I am a redeemed, forgiven, restored child of the King of kings, and His transforming power is constantly at work in my life, my relationships, my circumstances, my present and my future!"

If this increasingly becomes our default thinking and dialogue, our lives will begin to exude the presence and fragrance of our Lord Jesus Christ in any and every circumstance, and the "lord of the flies" will buzz off to some other putrefying place!

When Paul wrote to the Christians in Galatia about their tendency to revert to the past, he called them "foolish Galatians" and exhorted them with these words: *It is for freedom that Christ has set us free. Stand firm, then, and do not let yourselves be burdened again by a yoke of slavery (Galatians 5:1).*

How then should we respond when painful memories surface? We should speak truth to ourselves and to those memories!

The truth of God's complete and ongoing work of redemption in our lives;

the truth that He has indeed given us "beauty instead of ashes" and a "garment of praise instead of a spirit of despair";

the truth that He has removed our sins far from us, and that they no longer count against us;

the truth that the darkest corners of our hearts and lives now radiate with the glory of the abiding presence of God in us;

the truth that the very things that the enemy of our souls once intended for harm in our lives, God has redeemed and turned into something good and glorious;

the truth that the One who is eternal has bought back our past, present and future, and our lives now overflow with His peace, joy, expectant hope and divine purpose;

the truth that out of the trash heap in our lives, God has produced something that

is useful to His purposes

radiates with His glory

permeates the air with His fragrance

fills the atmosphere with the sweet song of His redemption...

The past is gone, the present is filled with abundant life, and the

future is glorious!

### What About You?

1. Have you fallen into the destructive habit of "stinkin' thinkin'" that has kept you depressed, oppressed, and full of unrest? Would you like to be free of this, and have your spirit uplifted and your step lightened?

2. Pray this commitment: "Lord I confess that I have allowed my thinking to become consumed with thoughts that do not reflect Your truth. With the help of Your precious Holy Spirit, I commit to the transformation of my mind by bringing my thoughts into alignment with the truth of Your Word, and the wonder of all You are."

3. For those who would like to engage in clear steps toward transforming toxic thinking, I would strongly recommend Dr. Caroline Leaf's book and program titled "Switch on Your Brain: The Key to Peak Happiness, Thinking, and Health". Information can be found on Dr. Leaf's website: drleaf.com

# CHAPTER 7
# SENSE AND CONSEQUENCE

*T*he past is gone...

*Therefore, there is now no condemnation for those who are in Christ Jesus, because through Christ Jesus the law of the Spirit of life set me free from the law of sin and death (Romans 8:1,2).*

These words are often glibly quoted – but what do they mean?

You have probably heard preachers say, "Whenever you read a "therefore" you need to look at what it's **there for!**"

This requires of us that we read the discussion that precedes the "therefore". In this instance, Paul, in writing to the church in Rome, explains that, under the law, we all stood under eternal condemnation before God because of our wrongdoing and rebellion against Him. However, since Jesus paid the penalty for our sin in our place, He has fulfilled the requirements of the law in our stead, on our behalf. Now, through repentance and receiving the free gift of God in Christ Jesus, we no longer stand condemned under that eternal penalty. Paul uses the word "condemnation" in its legal sense, as when in the context of court proceedings, a judge condemns a criminal to death – and says that we no longer stand under that condemnation before Him who is the Judge of all, because the Judge Himself has paid that penalty on our behalf!

Understanding this, we also need to ask the question, "What do these words **not** mean?"

It is sad to hear people use these words as a means of escaping their responsibilities, or as an excuse for avoiding accountability for their choices and actions, or to avoid "producing fruit in keeping with repentance" (Matthew 3:8, Luke 3:8). This is a misapplication of the scriptures, and grieves the Holy Spirit! Paul does not write these verses to mean that we get to escape the natural consequences of our choices and actions in this life!

If in the past I have made a poor choice to kill somebody, and subsequently come to repentance, God forgives me freely, and I no longer stand under His eternal judgment, because Christ has paid that penalty. However, I would still have to face the natural consequences of my actions in this life, and pay my penalty to society and the people I have injured.

In previous years I have had the joy of ministering to men formerly caught up in lifestyles of substance abuse and addiction. Their choices and decisions in life left a trail of destruction behind them – lost employment, broken families, financial debt, in trouble with the law, and sometimes homelessness... Finally, broken and at the end of themselves, they came to repentance and received God's forgiveness and new life in Jesus Christ. They became new creations, no longer under God's judgment.

However, this does not mean that they thereby escaped the consequences of the destruction they had sown through their previous choices. They could not say to their employers, wives, children, landlords, and law enforcers, "You don't understand! I'm a new creation now – the past is gone. God has forgiven me, and so should you – stop bringing up the past that God has forgiven!" This would be an all too convenient avoidance of their real responsibilities! They have to be held accountable for their own actions – otherwise they would never grow to manly maturity.

I have watched as these precious men have done the hard work of:

submitting to appropriate counsel, support and accountability in order to learn new, constructive patterns of behavior;

working at whatever employment they can initially find, to get started in earning a living; allocating a large portion of their wages to the back child support that has been accumulating for years;

working to rebuild trust with their spouses, children and employers;

doing what was required of them under the law, without blaming others for the things they had done...

and much more!

There are always one or two who resist this process. The financial and relational responsibilities seem overwhelming, and they resent being held accountable for their actions. At the heart of this lies a lack of true surrender to the Lordship of Jesus Christ. Instead of taking responsibility, they blame others. In doing so, they turn away from growing in Christian maturity, instead choosing to slide back into their old, destructive patterns of behavior.

It is true that God, as a free gift of His grace, does a supernatural work of transformation in our hearts. But from that point on, we need to learn how to live out this transformation in the practicalities of everyday life. In doing so, we do not remain passive while God does all the work for us! Instead, we cooperate with the Holy Spirit in learning and applying new behaviors that are reflective of our transformed hearts! The Bible calls this "sanctification" – and in Romans 12 – 14, Paul explains what that ongoing work of transformation through sanctification looks like:

In Romans 12:1 and 2, Paul tells us that it begins with

surrendering every part of our beings and lives to God as an act of worship;

no longer conforming to old patterns of thought and behavior;

renewing our minds (thinking and thought patterns) in a way that results in personal transformation.

The result, Paul goes on to say, is transformed patterns of attitudes and conduct:

sincerely loving others;

hating wrongdoing and not tolerating it in our own lives;

being spiritually enthusiastic;

being joyful, hopeful, patient, and faithful in prayer;

being hospitable;

being empathetic towards others – outwardly focused and seeing and understanding their needs, rather than being self-focused;

humility;

not being angry and vengeful, but rather one who brokers and facilitates peace;

honoring others above ourselves…

to name just a few!

Does this seem overwhelming? We very quickly realize that it takes discipline and accountability, and that our lives can only reflect such change with the help of the Holy Spirit's power!

1.  Discipline and accountability are reflections of God's love for us:

> *... the Lord disciplines those He loves, and He punishes everyone He accepts as a son. Endure hardship as discipline; God is treating you as sons... If you are not disciplined, then you are illegitimate children and not true sons... God disciplines us for our good, that we may share in His holiness. No discipline seems pleasant at the time, but painful. Later on, however, it produces a harvest of righteousness and peace for those who have been trained by it (Hebrews 12:6-11).*

We know that in the natural, it takes time, patience and hard work to produce a harvest. In the same way, it takes time, patience and work for us to produce the fruit of a transformed heart in our lives. If we balk at the process, that harvest will never come about, and the result will be ongoing brokenness in our circumstances and relationships.

In Ephesians 4:22-24, Paul talks about "putting off" the old self, and "putting on" the new self. Again, these are actions implying strenuous effort – not a passive "God will just do it for me" kind of attitude. Our new lives in Christ involve us cooperating with the work of the Holy Spirit in proactive ways, within the context of our loving relationship with Him.

Repentance means a one-hundred-and-eighty-degree change in our conduct: turning away from our old ways, and engaging in new, godly ways. Turning our backs on the trash of sin, and walking the walk of the "new creation" God has made us to be!

2.  The power of the Holy Spirit is activated in this process when we fully surrender to Him, and are willing to cooperate with His work in our hearts, minds and lives. This is what it means to *continue to work out your salvation in fear* (reverence) *and trembling (Philippians.2:12)*. As we surrender to, and cooperate with the power of the Holy Spirit in this way, we have the assurance that *it is God who works in you to will and act according to His good purpose (Philippians.2:13)*.

    Our God is a relational God. If He simply waved His hand and transformed our thoughts, attitudes and behaviors without our participation in the process, we would remain detached from Him – seeing Him as a distant, magical power to be harnessed at our command. But God is not a genie in a bottle! Rather, He brings us into partnership with Himself as Chief Executive Officer, in a family company called "God & Sons" and says, "Let's work on this construction project together! I will supply the power and the spiritual resources; all I need from you is your participation and engagement. As we work together, we will forge and deepen relationship with each other, and you will come to know Me in ways you never have before! This is what I delight in, my child, for you to know Me intimately as your daily reality!"

    Putting the past behind us - *forgetting what is behind,* as Paul phrases it - does not mean avoiding the unpleasant consequences of our choices. Instead it means turning away from those old, destructive choices, and making new, life-giving ones. Indeed, Paul goes on to talk about *straining ahead* and *pressing on* (Philippians 4:13, 14). As mentioned in a previous chapter, this calls for strenuous, committed effort on our part. He goes on to say, *all of us who are mature should take such a view of things* (4:15).

Part of that "straining ahead" entails continuing to put into practice the deeds of a transformed life. God freely forgives our sin, and freely redeems our pain and woundedness. But He also requires our committed cooperation in living out and walking in this redemption. Without this cooperation with the Holy Spirit, we run the grave risk of reverting to destructive ways, and consequently re-wounding ourselves and others.

God is indeed full of grace and mercy toward us, and does not treat us as our sins deserve. At the same time, like any good father, He desires for us to grow to strength and maturity. For that reason, in His great love, He trains us up in the way we should go.

Are you willing to take the hand of the Father and surrender to His discipline, so that the past can truly be left behind, and so that you can bear the fruit of a transformed life? It is through you and I making this new choice, that God fully redeems the seeds of destruction we have sown in the past. His discipline is loving – not harsh and full of condemnation and rage like some human fathers. We are safe in His hands, knowing that He only ever has our very best on His heart!

Surrender takes humility. The Bible says that God resists the proud, but gives grace to the humble (James 4:6). When we humble ourselves, God's grace comes right alongside of us in that most precious of all moments.

Surrender seems frightening when we contemplate it; but when we've yielded to it, oh what relief! What freedom! With what a lightened step we now walk!

---

### What About You?

1. Have you received Jesus as Savior for the forgiveness of your sins, but have resisted surrendering to Him as Lord, for the ongoing transformation of your thoughts, attitudes, and conduct?

2. Pray: "Lord I didn't even realize until just now, that I have not fully surrendered to You as Lord over my thoughts, attitudes, speech, choices, and actions. I invite You now, Holy Spirit, to continue to transform my heart, my mind, and my life, and I promise to co-operate with You as You guide me into all truth."

---

# CHAPTER 8
## LOSS AND GAIN

or the first forty years of my life I lived in South Africa, where I was born. It was there that I obtained my undergraduate and graduate qualifications, built my professional career and pursued a second occupation on the side, as a writer working in several genres, including short fiction for radio broadcast. Then I came to America and became a stranger among strangers.

Nobody knew about my academic achievements. Nobody knew about my professional accomplishments. Nobody had ever heard or read my stories. Nobody had ever heard of me… and nobody cared about any of this, except… me!

To exacerbate matters, South Africans of my generation were raised to be largely self-effacing and self-deprecating. Now, however, I was projected into a culture that was largely self-promoting. I felt like an insignificant ant being trampled by a legion of portentous elephants oblivious to my existence. Something new began to rise in me: a desire to make sure people understood just how educated, experienced, equipped and accomplished I was! I started making some feeble attempts at this self-promotion business. However, not only did this feel awkward and self-serving, but it came across that way too!

That was when I realized that I carried within me a form of "trash" I had never previously recognized – yet now I certainly seemed to be tripping over it at every step! It was the trash of my basic insecurity, and the trash of pride in my own achievements, abilities and career – and the fact that I had placed my identity in those things. What I **did** had become who I **was** – and when I came around people who neither knew or cared what I had done, I felt like a nobody and had a compelling need to correct this!

For the first time, the words of the apostle Paul in Philippians chapter 3 took on an immediacy for me. After listing his family heritage, his resume and his qualifications in the first part of the chapter, Paul then writes: *But whatever was to my profit I now consider loss for the sake of Christ. What is more, I consider everything a loss compared to the surpassing greatness of knowing Christ Jesus my Lord, for whose sake I have lost all things. I consider them* **rubbish** *(trash!), that I may gain Christ… (Philippians. 3:7-9a).*

The experience of being plunged into a new culture in a new country where I had no previous "history" or track-record, brought me face-to-face with the only reality of eternal consequence: that of knowing Jesus Christ. Inextricably intertwined with this is the immeasurable value of making Him known through my life – **Him** not myself or my "accomplishments"! It is His character, His renown, His glory revealed through my life, that matters – and that is transmittable across cultures, continents and lifetimes! And in Him I found my God-given identity – an identity that does not fluctuate with changing circumstances, relationships or occupations. Whether I am cleaning toilets or preaching to hundreds of people, I remain both the King's daughter and my Lord's servant!

Past achievements, while certainly useful as part of equipping for the present and future, are nevertheless "trash" compared to this truth: that I know and am known by the King of Kings and Lord of Lords! The One who spoke the universe into being; the One who continues to uphold that universe by His hand; the One who is radiant in the supremacy of His majesty and consuming in the embodiment of His love; the One who is overwhelming in the display of His power and the beauty of His holiness, and tender in the fullness of His compassion.

When **His** glory is revealed in and through you and me, academic degrees and job resumes and family lineage are embarrassingly paltry by comparison. Who can approach Him with these in our hands and claim superior stature on their basis? The idea is ludicrous!

Investing our identity in our academic qualifications, employment status, material possessions, and other transitory aspects of life, places us in a precarious position. Some twenty years ago, I spent six months on a "working vacation" in the alluring land of Scotland. There I helped to run the home and take care of the children of a couple well-known in the athletic world. Niall (not his real name) particularly, had a stellar career as a track athlete: he was an Olympic sprinter and gold-medalist. That is, until a devastating car accident almost cost him his life.

He was left with serious injuries and lasting disabilities that ended his athletic career. I remember the day he showed me the many medals he had won at the Commonwealth Games and the

Olympics. It was awe-inspiring to see and handle those trophies of an illustrious career. And yet... for Niall they represented nothing more than a lost past. Now he found himself having to forge a whole new identity. Before the accident, he had placed his identity in his status as a successful athlete. But that had been destroyed in one fateful, irretrievable moment. Once proudly on display for all to see, Niall's athletic medals were now stored out of sight in a velvet-lined box. Niall's daughter is now a world-class athlete who has won many medals herself. In a recent television interview with father and daughter, Niall affirmed that he still keeps his own medals stored away in that velvet-lined box all these many years later. They have become little more than relics of a lost identity.

In order to fully embrace the abundant life that God intended for us, we need to place our identity in something far more enduring than the fleeting circumstances and accomplishments of life[9]!

Pain and failure and loss in our lives are the "trash" that God redeems and transforms into something that puts His beauty on display. On the other hand, the successes and achievements in our lives often become our "treasures" that we pridefully parade for the sake of our own prestige. Yet how tawdry these seem compared to the majesty of God – like cheap toy vending machine costume jewelry compared to the brilliance of the Kimberley diamond!

What then, are we to do with these trophies of our lives? We are to take them down from the display cabinet, and put them in their rightful, surrendered place, as gracious gifts of a loving God, who delights to bless His children with good. Then we are to humbly

---

[9]      Teaching on our true, God-given identity has been thoroughly addressed in the book "True Identity" by Diane Fink of Aglow International, and in the "Destiny by Design" material by Gwen Bergquist of YWAM.

ask Him to instead put **Himself** on display in our lives. Humility attracts both God's attention and God's presence. He will answer that prayer – and the result will be a life that radiates His beauty and glory more than ever before.

One of my personal heroes is a man I knew as a child in Durban, South Africa. He was a Zulu pastor named William Duma, whose ministry was marked by an extraordinary power of God[10]. The secret of this power was a man of deep humility who spent hours "knowing God" in the intimacy of prayer. Every time he stood up to preach, he breathed the words, "Take Your glory, Lord". In other words, may Jesus be on display, not William Duma. I have since adopted these words as my own personal "motto".

In Isaiah 42:8 we read these words: *"I am the Lord; that is my name! I will not give my glory to another or my praise to idols"*.

What are the "trophies" (idols) you have on display in your life?

Your family heritage?

Your education?

Your material possessions?

Your career accomplishments?

Your independence and self-sufficiency?

Your social connections?

Can you count your family heritage as "loss" in exchange for being known as a son or daughter of the King of kings and a servant in His kingdom?

Can you count your education as "trash" compared to the immeasurable greatness of knowing the One who is Himself the power and wisdom of God (1 Corinthians 1:24)?

---

[10] You can read his story in the book "Take Your Glory Lord" by Mary Garnett

Can you count your material possessions as inconsequential compared to your treasure in heaven stored up through a life lived for the Kingdom of God?

Can you count your career accomplishments as "loss" compared to the eternal purposes of God fulfilled through your life?

Can you count your independence and self-sufficiency as "trash" in exchange for deep dependence on Jesus Christ and His life at work in you?

Can you count your social connections as inconsequential compared to having gained Christ and being "found in Him" (Philippians.3:9)?

Pride in position, accomplishments, possessions and connections, leads to a constant need for recognition, affirmation and even adulation. The result is jealousy, insecurity, being territorial and competitive, and constantly comparing ourselves with others. It does not take a great deal of insight to discern that this leaves little room for the glory of God to be revealed through a life! These attitudes clutter up our innermost beings with... trash!

James 4:6 reminds us, *"God opposes the proud but gives grace to the humble"*.

On the other hand, feelings of inferiority, unworthiness, self-criticism and self-rejection hinder us from fully living out all that God created us to be – and thereby also leave little room for His glory to be displayed.

The psalmist writes, *"For you created my inmost being... I praise you because I am fearfully and wonderfully made..."* (Psalm 139:13, 14) and Paul tells Timothy, *Everything God created is good, and nothing is to be rejected... (1 Timothy 4:4)*. We are stamped with the

Manufacturer's seal of approval! Do you want the grace of God to so overflow your life that wherever you go and whoever you meet, His grace on you and in you and through you is immediately evident? Then you need to reach the decision that the apostle Paul made: *But whatever was to my profit I now consider loss for the sake of Christ (Philippians.3:7).*

Jesus is the greatest treasure – and in considering all else loss in exchange for the glory of "being found in Him", lies our greatest gain. The result for us is, once again, a life that shines with His own radiance – a radiance that far outlasts and outshines family heritage and brilliant careers and beautiful houses and stellar accomplishments.

God said these words to Abraham: *"...I am your shield, your very great reward" (Genesis.1:15).* When we gain Him, we no longer need or crave human accolades, rewards, or awards. In fact, God also gave Abraham this promise: *"I will make your name great, and you will be a blessing" (Genesis. 12:2).* The greatest "reputation" we can aspire to, is that of the life and love and grace of Jesus spilling from our lives to touch and bless the lives of others in His name.

*"Whoever believes in Me, as Scripture has said, rivers of living water will flow from within them" (John 7:38).*

We live in a particularly narcissistic culture and generation. From "selfies" to obsessive self-exploration to self-promotion, we are caught up in an endless riptide of self-focus. And the consequences for both our relationship with God and our relationships with one another, are as destructive as any rip-current. We have been bedazzled by the Hollywood mindset of "star power". No wonder then that the manifestation of the glory of God has faded. We have been too focused on putting ourselves on display, rather than hungering for Him to be revealed through us.

One of my previous students told me of the following experience she had, and gave me permission to tell her story: A gifted communicator, she had a desire to preach and speak publicly. One night she had a dream that she had just finished speaking to a huge audience that filled a vast auditorium. The audience had leapt to their feet, and were applauding long and loudly, and she stood on the platform, basking in the adulation. However, while the standing ovation continued, she had the strange feeling that something or someone was behind her. Trying not to make it too obvious that she was sneaking a look, she peeked over her shoulder. And this is what she saw: standing behind her and towering over her, brilliant with radiance, was Jesus – and the audience was applauding Him, not her!

Oh what a sobering reminder that the only One worthy of being on display in our lives, is Jesus!

These are just a few of the things the Bible has to say about boasting:

*Through Him we have gained access by faith into this grace in which we now stand. And we boast in the hope of the glory of God... Not only is this so, but we also boast in God through our Lord Jesus Christ (Romans 5:2, 11).*

*Let the one who boasts, boast in the Lord (1 Corinthians 1:31, 2 Corinthians 10:17).*

*May I never boast except in the cross of our Lord Jesus Christ, through which the world has been crucified to me, and I to the world (Galatians 6:14).*

*For it is by grace that you have been saved, through faith — and this is not from yourselves, it is a gift of God — not by works, so that no one can boast. For we are God's handiwork, created in Christ Jesus to do good works, which God prepared in advance for us to do (Ephesians 2:8-10).*

May not only our words, but also our lives, constantly boast of Him who is the "radiance of the Father's glory"!

*And we, who with unveiled faces all reflect the Lord's glory, are being transformed into his likeness with ever-increasing glory, which comes from the Lord, who is the Spirit (2 Corinthians. 3:18).*

Let us shine with and for **Him!**

## What About You?

1. Have you placed your identity or your reputation in your connections or accomplishments, your possessions or position, your lineage or your legacy? Has this resulted either in self-focused pride, or in insecurity and inferiority?

2. Pray: "Lord I acknowledge that I have been trying to base my identity or my reputation on things that are superficial and fleeting. I repent of this, and pray now, as did John the Baptist in speaking of You, that I would decrease that You may increase. May You be made known in and through me, for You are my most precious treasure."

# CHAPTER 9
# WHOLE HEARTED

My dog is a German Shepherd/Border Collie mix. He is a non-stop energy machine. He has been with me since he was eight weeks old, and I have consistently fed him, played with him, walked and run and hiked with him, and taken him almost everywhere with me in the car unless the weather is too hot. He sleeps on the floor beside my bed at night, and he wakes with me each morning.

Anyone observing my relationship with my dog would come to conclusion that he trusts me. And he does... up to a point...

He has a variety of toys with which he loves to play fetch: several balls in different shapes and sizes, a couple of Frisbees, and a few tug ropes. Whenever I throw a ball or Frisbee, and he fetches it and brings it back to me, I always throw it for him again - and at the end of every game he gets to keep his toy. Yet his doggy brain seems to be in a constant state of suspicion that if he gives me the ball or Frisbee, he may never get it back again. Consequently, each time I throw a toy, he runs to fetch it, and then... he dives into his "den" under the tree house and stashes it there. Then he waits for me to throw the next one. This continues until he has collected all his toys under the tree house, and then he crawls in there and lies on top of them, so that I can't take them away!

However, this behavior changes completely when I have a treat in my hand. Then he dashes after the toy, comes running back with it at full speed, and drops it at my feet in exchange for a treat. No matter how much I try to teach him to bring the ball back anytime I throw it, he will only do so when he expects to get something better in return!

Recently my dog injured his paw. He was limping on that leg, and constantly licking and worrying at this bothersome paw. Concerned for his pain and distress, I longed to help him and provide relief. But each time I tried to take a look at this paw in order to identify the problem and address it, he would grab my hand in his mouth and pull it away. He wanted help, but he did not completely trust me with his hurt.

Watching these behaviors in my dog has made me realize that you and I demonstrate the same tendencies in our relationship with God. He is with us always. He never leaves us, never abandons us. He is our protector and provider, the One who full of goodness is His character, the One whose intentions toward us are always good all the time. The One of whom the Scriptures say, *He heals the brokenhearted and binds up their wounds (Psalm 147:3).*

It is interesting to read in the book of Exodus chapter 33, that when Moses asked of God, "Show me Your glory," God responded by saying, *"I will cause all my **goodness** to pass in front of you..."* *(Exodus 33:18, 19).*

We often think of God's glory as something overwhelming, evoking our reverence – and there is truth in this. But do we realize that God most often reveals His glory to us in the form of His **goodness?** His intentions towards us, and His working in our lives is consistently good and only ever for our good! And as part of that goodness, our broken hearts are safe in His healing hands.

And yet...

No matter how many times we cry out to Him to heal our lacerated hearts, no matter how we plead with Him for His mercy poured out into our lives and circumstances, no matter how intensely we long for Him to redeem and restore all that is lost and broken in our lives... Somewhere in the depths of our hearts a suspicion lurks, that He cannot be completely trusted. Consequently, even while praying these prayers, we stop short of **giving** Him our whole hearts.

We want Him to **make** our hearts, our lives whole. But we refuse to **give** Him our whole hearts, our whole lives. Perhaps we are willing to do so only conditionally: if in exchange we can get some visible proof of guarantee that it is going to turn out to be both safe and beneficial, before we will relinquish our hearts and lives to Him.

God never forces anything on us. While He may allow circumstances that might motivate us to fully relinquish our hearts and lives to Him, He will never forcibly wrest them from us. And so we are left with a dilemma: **God can not heal, redeem and restore those parts of our hearts and lives that we withhold from Him and refuse to give Him!**

If you and I truly want God to heal our broken hearts and lives and make them whole, and redeem and restore every lost and broken part, then we have to **give** Him our whole hearts, our whole lives, relinquishing, surrendering and abandoning them to Him in every part. Only then does God have full access to all that is broken and wounded and hurting, in order to make it whole and new and shining with His radiance.

It all comes down to trust. Do you trust Him? Do you have unshakeable confidence in His character, in His intentions toward you, in both His power and His willingness to *work all things together for good* in your heart and life?

So many times I hear people say, "Well I prayed, but God didn't…" When we pray and ask God to accomplish what only He can do, yet withhold parts of our hearts and lives from Him, we are saying to Him, "My will, not Yours be done. Just do what I want God, and I want to stay in control while You're doing it, because I want to make sure that all is done my way."

Then when we don't get what we want, the way we want it, in the time we want it in, we conclude that God and His Word do not "work" and that we therefore need to find our answers elsewhere. In the end we demonstrate greater trust in various human modalities and methodologies than we ever have in God, all the while casting aspersions on His power and willingness to be the Healer of our hearts.

Do you long for God to heal your broken heart and make it whole? If so, it is time to stop holding out on Him. It is time to take a step of deep trust in the One who loves you with a fathomless, unending love, and say, "Lord, I give all to You: all that I am and all that I have. All my desires, disappointments, wounds, needs, hopes, dreams. I relinquish myself to You who are Lord and lover of my heart and soul, and release not only my circumstances, but my very being to You to accomplish those things that only You are able to do by Your power."

*Trust Him at all times, you people; pour out your hearts to Him, for God is our refuge (Psalm 62:8).*

*I have sought Your face with all my heart; be gracious to me according to Your promise (Psalm 119:58).*

*Trust in the Lord with all your heart and lean not on your own understanding (Proverbs 3:5).*

The Word of God urges us to surrender all of our hearts trustingly to Him, rather than placing our hope, trust and reliance in human reasoning, rationale, psychology, methodology, strategy, competency, or creativity. These things may well be useful tools at times – but they are not our primary resource for healing. We make a tragic mistake when we place our primary trust in these, and then attempt to use God as a supplementary "tool" to bolster this choice. God is a supernatural God who works according to His supernatural nature – not according to our puny, limited intellect and views. The human brain is not able to fully understand the workings of the human brain – let alone the workings of the eternal, supernatural, Almighty God! It is supreme arrogance to apply our human intellect in determining what God can and cannot, will and will not, should and should not do!

He **is** Lord! If we do not live our lives surrendered in every part to His lordship, this certainly unbalances our own lives – but it does not deprive Him of continuing to be who He is in His being. We become the losers, endlessly, restlessly trying to find satisfaction through other people, relationships, or methodologies we have enthroned in our lives – a lifelong quest doomed to futility.

There is a deep, endless, bountiful, satisfying well and wealth to be had and experienced in the One who loves us with a consuming passion. He is utterly trustworthy – worthy of our trust. He is lover and healer of our hearts, redeemer and restorer of our lives.

In the words of one of my favorite songs, "Your love never fails, never gives up, never runs out on me[11]".

Whenever I think of abandoning myself wholly to the Lord, I envisage a picture of a little girl (or boy) standing on a wall, and calling to her Dad, "Catch me, Daddy!"

Dad opens his arms, and the little one abandons herself trustingly to the arms of her father, and jumps. And he always catches her, never lets her fall.

The loving, mighty arms of the Father are wide open to you. Will you trust Him? Will you launch yourself from the "safety" of whatever "wall" you have been relying on, and jump into His arms? He will catch you; He will hold you; He will never, ever let you fall.

Sometimes difficulty in trusting our heavenly Father stems from past wounding in our relationship with our earthly fathers. If your human father sent you mixed messages, meted out conditional love, let you down in significant ways, abandoned, rejected, neglected or abused you, was inconsistent, distant and disinterested, or betrayed you, you may project those experiences of what your human father was like, onto your perception of God as Father.

---

[11]    One Thing Remains: Bethel Music Publishing

However, God as Father is nothing like the human father who failed you! His love for you is consistent and persistent, it does not fluctuate in its intensity and commitment, it is deep and lavish, it is protective and nurturing and life-giving, it is kind and compassionate and solid and reliable. Not long before He was crucified, Jesus' disciples, having long observed Him talk to and about the Father, finally asked, *"Show us the Father."* Jesus answered with these words, *"If you have seen Me, you have seen the Father" (John 14:8, 9)*.

If we want to know what God is like as Father, we need look no further than Jesus! See Him reach out in compassion, and healing, and forgiveness, and infinite love and grace and mercy as He walked through the mess of broken humanity. Hear His words as He says of Himself, quoting Isaiah 61: *He (the Father) has sent Me to bind up the brokenhearted, to proclaim freedom for the captives and release from darkness for the prisoners… to comfort all who mourn… to bestow on them a crown of beauty instead of ashes, the oil of joy instead of mourning, and a garment of praise instead of a spirit of despair.*

In Exodus 15:26, God says this of Himself: *"…I am the Lord who heals you"*, while Psalm 34:18 assures us, *The Lord is close to the brokenhearted and saves those who are crushed in spirit.*

It is His nature to tenderly heal the hearts of His children – not to further hurt them. We need not withhold any part of ourselves from Him. Our hearts are safe in His love, in His keeping. The word used in the Bible for God as Father, is the Aramaic word *Abba* – the word still used by children in addressing their Dads in Arabic languages today. It simply means "Daddy", and it denotes a relationship of sweet, trusting, dependent intimacy.

Our heart's secrets, wounds, hopes, and dreams are safe with Him. Once again, I urge you: *Trust Him at all times, you people; pour out your hearts to Him, for God is our refuge (Psalm 62:8).*

---

### What About You?

1. Have you been withholding a part of your own heart from God, out of fear that He will somehow let you down?

2. If you are willing to entrust your heart to the deep love of your heavenly Father, pray this prayer: "Heavenly Father, I confess that I have been holding part of my heart back from You out of fear. I ask that You would heal those wounded places in me that cause me to regard You with distrust. I entrust my heart to You now, and pray that You will drench my heart with Your love, and make me whole."

---

# CHAPTER 10
# I SURRENDER ALL...

"I just want you to know I'm not staying!"

These were the first words out of my mouth as I got into my parents' car at the airport in Seattle. I had just arrived off a flight from Johannesburg, South Africa. I love South Africa, and living in the United States permanently was not in my vision for my future.

That was over sixteen years ago! For the two years following this adamant declaration, I became more and more unhappy with every attempt to make things come out my way. I wrestled and wrangled and strategized and manipulated and became more and more angry. Then one night as I stood in a prayer meeting at the church I attended, I heard a still, small voice say "It's time to give up."

And so I did! Oh I did not give up in the sense of throwing in the towel. Rather, I stopped resisting God. I yielded to Him, abandoning myself to His sovereignty over my life. Immediately it was as if a great encumbrance rolled off my shoulders – and along with the new lightness in my step came an inner joy. Surrender to God is a relief! I no longer needed to wrestle, wrangle, strategize and manipulate. Instead I could trust every step of my way to the One who holds all of my life in His hands.

The curious thing is... if anyone had asked me, prior to my arrival in the United States, whether my life was completely surrendered to the Lord, I would have said "Yes!" It took a specific set of circumstances to bring into the light the truth that I wanted to remain at the controls in certain areas at all times. Unknowingly, I had been saying, "Lord, You can have everything else, but not this. This is non-negotiable. In this area, Lord, not Your will, but **mine** be done!"

In the years that followed this revelation, I have come to realize that throughout our lives we are presented with multiple opportunities for further and deeper surrender. On every occasion, the core question is: "Who/what is really Lord of my life?"

Not only do we need to entrust our whole hearts to Him, but **God can only redeem our experiences and circumstances to the extent that we are surrendered to Him as Lord.** Submitting ourselves, our experiences and our circumstances to Him, positions us under His authority, and gives Him open access to work His power in our lives. But if we continue to either want to remain in control ourselves, or if someone or something other than God reigns supreme in our lives, God's redemptive work is hindered. God is a relational God who works in partnership with us, and respects our free will.

He is not truly Lord of our lives if we are governed by:

- Our own feelings and emotions – acting on the way we feel, rather than in response to the Word of God;

- Our own stubborn willfulness and determination – insisting that things be accomplished according to our will, our way and our timeline;
- Another person, methodology or philosophy we are enamored with – and so tailoring our thinking, decisions and actions to align with those rather than with the Word of God;
- A worldview or belief system that is in opposition to the Word of God – so that we are drinking at a fountain other than that of the Living Water;
- Our own opinions – relying on our own reasoning powers rather than trusting in the Him and the truth of His Word;
- Or, as was the case with me, anything we withhold from Him, regarding it as "non-negotiable".

If God is truly Lord of our lives, then our
prayers
actions
thoughts
motivations
attitudes
goals
energies
will be governed by and directed towards the expression and accomplishment of **His** purposes in and through our
lives
circumstances
activities
relationships.

No matter what the circumstances look like; no matter what desires stir in our hearts, our single-minded focus would be living a life out of the core surrender of our will and desires to His will, His way, His timing, His purpose.

On the other hand, if in practice something or someone else is lord in our lives, then our

prayers

actions

thoughts

motivations

attitudes

goals

energies

would be directed towards trying to get both God and others to serve the purpose of that person, relationship, aspiration, possession, activity or ideal that holds preeminence in our lives. Instead of trusting God with this area of our greatest priority, our

physical

mental

emotional

spiritual

attention and energies will be consumed with trying to get God and others to help accomplish what we want in this area of our most intense focus.

The destructive effects of this state of affairs are widespread:

You devalue your relationship with God, "using" Him to serve your own lesser "lord".

You devalue your relationships with others, "using" them similarly, reducing their intrinsic worth in your life to the extent to which they help you serve this priority also. Both God and others become expendable when it seems they are no longer serving your purpose.

You expend your own energies towards who or what is "lord" in your life to an extent that begins to destroy you from the inside out.

You sacrifice your God-given identity and destiny on the altar of your "lord".

You sacrifice the fullness of God's glorious purposes in and through your life, on this same altar.

Can you just let go? Can you release the person, relationship, aspiration, possession, activity, goal or ideal you hold so tightly in your cramped fist, and relinquish yourself as well as him, her or it to the Lordship of Jesus Christ? Can you trust that God in His consuming love, wisdom and faithfulness is at all times working for your highest and best good — so that the abundance of His life will cause you to flourish?

Or are you determined to maintain your grip on your lesser "lord", continuing to exist in a sad wilderness of wilted potential while you strive for what can never truly satisfy your deepest longings?

It is significant that in almost every instance in Scripture where God is referred to as Redeemer, He is simultaneously referred to as Lord. In order to experience His redeeming power and work in our lives, we need to first surrender completely to His lordship, abandoning ourselves to His loving authority.

To choose the Lordship of Jesus Christ in our lives is to choose life. To choose the Lordship of Jesus Christ is to choose to trust Him to cause us to flourish and thrive. To choose the Lordship of Jesus Christ is to choose to live our lives out of a place of freedom, authority, healing, redemption, restoration and joy.

To choose the Lordship of Jesus Christ is to make way for His redeeming power to be released in every part of our lives and circumstances!

Psalm 103 says this: *Bless the **Lord** o my soul... who **redeems** your life from the pit and crowns you with love and compassion, **who satisfies you with good things** so that your youth is renewed like the eagle's (v. 4, 5).*

In the original Hebrew, the literal translation of the word "pit" in our English Bible, is "ruin". He redeems our lives from every imaginable kind of ruin.

Because we live in a fallen, broken world, we all have experiences of "ruin" in one way or another. When we worship God as Lord of our lives, He redeems those "ruinous" experiences, and instead of being marked by them, we become people marked by His love and compassion.

In the Amplified Bible, verse 5 reads this way: *Who satisfies your necessity and desire **at your personal age and situation** with good so that your youth, renewed, is like the eagle's — strong, overcoming, soaring!*

This verse tells us that God's redemptive work in our lives is not a "one size fits all" deal. Rather it is very individual and specific, tailored for each person in each unique set of circumstances. We can trust His Lordship — His authority, sovereignty and power — because He is always working redemptively with our good in mind. The result is that our lives are revitalized and re-energized. Instead of feeling helpless and hopeless, we have fresh purpose and reason to live!

To surrender completely to Jesus as Lord, is to abandon ourselves to Him in trust, relinquishing our unwarranted suspicions of His faithfulness and intentions toward us.

Then, with the psalmist, we too can say, *I am still confident of this: I will see the goodness of the Lord in the land of the living. Wait for the Lord; be strong and take heart and wait for the Lord (Psalm 27:13, 14).*

<u>What About You?</u>

1. Have you been stubbornly holding out for God to accomplish YOUR will in your life and circumstances?

2. If you are willing to surrender to His Lordship in every area, entrusting yourself to His love and good purposes, pray this prayer: "Lord, I surrender. I acknowledge that I have been trying to be the one in control, expecting You to do things my way. I choose now to relinquish my own will, and surrender every part of myself and my life to Your Lordship, Your sovereignty, Your power, Your love, and Your good purposes."

# CHAPTER 11
# A TALE OF TWO FRIENDS

*T*wo friends. Two circumstances. Two responses. Two outcomes.

These are both people I knew many years ago, in South Africa. The first friend, who I shall call Tammy, had been active for a number of years in the church that I attended. She had come from a very broken past, and before and after the birth of her first child, painful memories began to surface with insistent frequency. From time to time Tammy would call me in the depths of the night hours when she could not sleep, and I would listen while she sobbed and screamed out her pain over the phone.

Although there was excellent Christian counseling easily available to her, Tammy became very enamored with a practitioner of a methodology that incorporated humanistic and New Age ideas and practices. She began at first to dabble, and then progressively immerse herself deeper in this methodology. When she was warned by others in the church as to the pitfalls of this, she would become annoyed and defensive, and say, "I know what I'm doing". Gradually she isolated herself more and more from fellow believers, and ultimately bounced from one New Age practice to the next, each time becoming more deeply enmeshed and increasingly self-absorbed.

Ultimately she closed her ears and her heart to the Word of God, and her choices left a trail of destruction and confusion behind her, in her personal relationships. Hers became a quest unrequited, always seeking, always absorbed with excavating her own inner landscape, always restless and dissatisfied in a pursuit without end. Yet she remained convinced that she knew what she was doing.

Far from her painful past being redeemed, further wounding and ceaseless searching have attended the path that Tammy chose to follow.

Not too long after Tammy started on this tragic journey, I met another friend, Celeste (her real name). From well before I met her, and continuing for a number of years following, Celeste experienced recurring heartache and pain in one trauma and tragedy after another. I have yet to meet anyone else who has gone through so much unrelenting heartbreak over such a protracted period. Even I was overwhelmed, just witnessing all that she experienced.

Yet through every circumstance, Celeste made one consistent choice: to run toward the Lord with all her pain and devastation; to cling to Him in desperate and childlike trust; to bury herself ever more deeply into His love. Through these piercingly painful years, I saw a transformation take place in Celeste: she began to glow with such a profound radiance, that we began to call her "our Celestial friend"!

I have yet to meet anyone in life as radiant as my friend Celeste.

And then… as she honored Him with her life, I saw God begin to redeem every tragic and painful experience Celeste had endured. What is more, from her life flowed a fruitfulness that continues to bring freedom to the lives of countless others blessed to come within her orbit.

In our own times of pain, we are faced with several interconnected choices:

- To turn with desperation-driven fervency towards God, or to take steps along a path that leads away from Him;
- To cling to the truth of His Word, or to abandon it in favor of alternative "feel-good" ideas that provide immediate gratification;
- To trust Him no matter what, or to transfer our trust to someone or something else;
- To look to Him, or to turn our gaze inward;
- To wait trustingly for His redemptive purposes to be worked out, or to make our own arrangements, based on our own reasoning and strategizing.

In making these choices, the core issue is what we believe about God's love for us. God's trustworthiness is based on His character. However, it is also true that we can only trust where we know we are truly loved. So the point at which we have trouble trusting that God can and will redeem all of our "trash", is the point at which we have trouble believing His profound love for us.

In the closing verses of Ephesians 3, Paul articulates this prayer for the believers in Ephesus: *I pray that out of His glorious riches He may strengthen you with power through His Spirit in your inner being, so that Christ may dwell in your hearts through faith. And I pray that you, being rooted and established in love, may have power, together with all the saints, to grasp how wide and long and high and deep is the love of Christ, and to know this love that surpasses knowledge – that you may be filled to the measure of all the fullness of God (Ephesians 3:16-19).*

Then Paul continues in verse 20: ***Now** to Him who is able to do immeasurably more than all we ask or imagine, according to His power that is at work within us...*

Note the sequence as expressed in these verses:

1. The strengthening power of the Holy Spirit works deeply inside of us, producing faith that opens our hearts for Christ to dwell there;
2. Through this faith, we become firmly rooted in the love of Christ, personally experiencing the reality of the love of Christ more and more – a love that is solid and reliable, and outstrips anything we have ever known before;
3. As we experience more of His love, we become increasingly filled with all that God is;
4. Resulting in our growing confidence that God is able and willing to accomplish more than we could imagine in our wildest dreams – and to do so according to **His** power at work **within us.**

The starting place is opening ourselves to the work of the Holy Spirit in our lives, leading to strengthening faith and experiencing God's profound love, and resulting in an intimate relationship whereby we partner with God's power in the supernatural accomplishment of His all-surpassing redemptive purposes!

This amazing work of God prompts Paul to burst into spontaneous praise: *To Him be glory in the church and in Christ Jesus throughout all generations, for ever and ever!*

What a dynamic and glorious contrast to what the purveyors of humanism/psychology/new age have on offer: that of lifelong bondage to the never-ending, fruitless excavation of our own inner landscape. We will never find definitive freedom and healing by continually digging into ourselves – either alone or with the intervention of another person! The only One truly capable of reaching deeply into the innermost recesses of our beings and drawing off the poison and excavating trash for the purpose of healing us from its infected wounds, delivering us from its destruction, cleansing us from its mess, and redeeming us from its bondage, is the Spirit of the living God!

Proverbs 20:27 – *The lamp of the Lord searches the spirit of a man; it searches out his inmost being.*

1 Corinthians 2:10 – *The Spirit searches all things, even the deep things of God.*

Note how Paul describes the characteristics of the love of Christ:

His love is *wide*: This refers to the limitless capacity of God's love. His love extends to embrace all that we are or ever will be, all that we have experienced and ever will experience, with all of His heart.

His love is *long*: It is lasting. God's love does not fade or falter along the way, or fall short. It outlasts the entire length of our life's journey, all the way to eternity. Whatever long road we may travel, God's love is long-lasting enough to accompany us and go before us all the long way, and will be waiting to greet and embrace us when the journey is done.

His love is *high*: It is higher than any other love we can ever experience. It is pure and uncontaminated and unconditional and without hidden agendas. It is flawless and faultless and unfailing.

His love is *deep*: It reaches into places in us that nothing and no one else could ever touch. It seeps into the deepest recesses of our hearts and spirits and beings, to the very essence of who we are. It completes us and satisfies us and fills us and draws us into the very depths of God Himself. There is nothing in the universe that can come anywhere close to matching the love of God! It is fathomless – beyond any human experience or comprehension.

How tragic then, that so often those who are willing to open themselves deeply to practitioners of therapies that project anti-Biblical ideologies, and to diligently follow their methodologies, are unwilling to open themselves just as deeply to the love and Holy Spirit of God, or to just as diligently apply His Word in and to their lives! There is nothing lacking in the power of God and His Word, to bring about all the transformation and restoration we need in any area or circumstance of our lives. His work is a complete work – if we will only open and surrender ourselves to Him, putting our trust in Him completely.

In Psalm 130, the psalmist writes: ...*put your hope in the Lord, for with the Lord is unfailing love and with Him is **full** redemption.*

**Full** redemption! Nothing is left out, nothing is overlooked, nothing is forgotten, nothing falls by the wayside in God's redemptive Kingdom economy!

What are your circumstances? What is your response? What will the outcome of your life be? Will you choose to treat God like an experiment yet to be proved, hedging your bets by nibbling here and there at this —ology and that —ism, always searching, yet never finding the answers you crave, and never being able to fill the hunger that gnaws at you?

In writing to Timothy, Paul describes those who do this as *having a form of godliness, but denying its power (2 Timothy 3:5)* and as *always learning but never able to acknowledge the truth (2 Timothy 3:7).*

James tells us that *he who doubts is like a wave of the sea, blown and tossed by the wind... (James 1:6).*

Or... will your response be to cast yourself on the Lord in trusting surrender to His great power and love, burying yourself deeper and deeper into Him, giving Him your whole heart, and opening the depths of your being to all that He is?

It is in this response that we experience the profound love of the Lord for us, and make our lives available to the fullness of His power and the fulfillment of His divine purposes in and through our lives.

My prayer for you is the one Paul prayed for the Ephesian believers: *... that out of His glorious riches He may strengthen you with power through His Spirit in your inner being, so that Christ may dwell in your hearts through faith. And I pray that you, being rooted and established in love, may have power, together with all the saints, to grasp how wide and long and high and deep is the love of Christ, and to know this love that surpasses knowledge – that you may be filled to the measure of all the fullness of God. Now to Him who is able to do immeasurably more than all we ask or imagine, according to His power* *that is at work within us, to Him be glory in the church and in Christ Jesus throughout all generations, for ever and ever!*

In Him is **full** redemption!

---

### What About You?

1. In what ways have you struggled to trust God's love for you?

2. Pray: "Lord I need a fresh revelation of Your love to my heart. I don't ask you for PROOF of Your love – You have already proved it on the cross. But as I purpose to open my heart fully to You now, I ask that You would bathe all of my being in Your love so deeply, that I will never be the same again."

---

# CHAPTER 12
# NEWBORNS WALKING

*T*o walk, and then… to run!

Some sixteen years ago, I volunteered in a home for abandoned babies, in Johannesburg, South Africa. Volunteers were essential to the work of the home, because finances were sparse, and not enough full-time, paid staff could be hired.

As a result of the shortage of full-time staff, babies were often left in their cribs for extended periods of each day. Staff members often only had just enough time to feed, bathe and change each infant. There was little or no time for any further interaction: babies were rarely held or played with. Consequently, these babies, while they did learn to pull themselves up inside their cribs, did not learn to crawl or walk normally. Eventually it was necessary for a volunteer physical therapist to come and work with them, to help them catch up with these milestones. Volunteer caregivers like me also began to provide supplementary interaction with each baby.

The Bible frequently talks about our lives in Christ in terms of new birth, rebirth, new creation, etc. Yet it is curious that we so often fail to see the analogy between physical and spiritual birth.

Usually when a baby is born into a family, we don't say, "How exciting! Lovely baby!" — and then leave the baby to his or her own devices, to fend for himself while we go about our business. The new baby needs to be fed, clothed, taught, and have her diapers changed; she needs to be helped to learn how to walk and talk, supported as he or she grows to maturity, and yes, disciplined.

Similarly, a spiritual "new creation" does not achieve spiritual maturity alone! He or she needs other, loving Christian believers to help him grow and learn. It is an active process requiring participation and interaction in the context of relationship:

Pastors, teachers and mentors to feed and nurture him in the word of God;

Wise and godly counselors to teach him how to live out the transformed life — how to "put off" the old self and "put on" the new;

Loving brothers and sisters to support and encourage and share in mutually beneficial authentic relationship...

When these things do not happen, the "new creation" becomes stunted in his or her spiritual development, and then strenuous intervention is required to make up for this lack!

In the same way, when we are newly healed and delivered from past brokenness, pain and sin, we need the support and engagement of other, mature believers, to learn to "walk" in our new healing and freedom!

Several years ago, I fractured my heel in two places, tore ligaments throughout my foot, and bruised my Achilles tendon. Recovery time from heel fractures is considerable, and the process complicated, and so a splint boot and crutches became my new fashion accessories for three months. When I was finally able to relinquish these, an activity I had taken for granted all my life, now had to be relearned. I had to learn to walk normally again!

What had been broken was now healed – but I had to learn to use those muscles and operate those joints and stretch those tendons and ligaments all over again. What is more, I needed a program to follow, and ideally, someone to supervise that program and monitor my progress. Why? Because an improperly rehabilitated injury like this would cause a change in my gait, which in turn would cause further injury to knees, hips, back...

This picture of healing and rehabilitation has a spiritual parallel: When Jesus has healed our broken past, we then need to learn how to walk in our newly found wholeness. Walking in woundedness causes further injury to both ourselves and others, leading to further destruction. Trained, Bible-based, Christ-centered Christian counselors and mentors are God's gift to us at such times. They are able to help us relinquish behaviors that might keep us crippled, and teach us how to exercise new, wholesome behaviors instead, until these become strong enough to be our healthy "new normal". Such counselors can give us caring guidance in how to "put off the old man" and take on the life of the "new man" so that the past remains behind us, and no longer encroaches on or contaminates our future.

Increasingly, the "new man" becomes our new way of living, and we continue to grow stronger and stronger in this. Gradually I relinquished my crutches, and needed to do my rehabilitation exercises with decreasing frequency, as my walking ability normalized. In the same way, as we grow stronger in our new, spiritual walk, we may need the help of a counselor or resource person less and less until we become strong enough to walk in newness of life without their help.

Not long after I first injured my foot, I also became ill. I was running a high fever, had a terrible headache, was full of body aches, and felt very weak. That week, in conversation with a friend, I suddenly could not remember the American terms and pronunciation for many words and expressions. Although I had come to the United States from South Africa over twelve years prior to this, in a state of physical stress and weakness I forgot what I had learned of my new home, and reverted to old, familiar, South African expressions and vocabulary. Fortunately my friend, who knows me very well, not only understood me, but was able to supply what I lacked.

Life is stressful! No matter how strong we have become in our walk, in moments of stress and distress particularly, we can "forget" what we have learned, and revert to some old, familiar ways. It is then that we need our fellow brothers and sisters in Christ, to come alongside of us with their understanding, to lend us their strength, and remind us of our new, God-given life and vocabulary.

God never intended us to walk this walk alone. The Scriptures are filled with "one another" verses. The family of God is essential to our ongoing strength along the way. As we each grow stronger, we find that not only are we strengthened **by** our fellow believers, but we in turn can provide strength **to** others also.

In my own life, I have taught at a Bible college for the past twelve years and more, where I have the privilege of mentoring and discipling students of all ages. Yet so many of those same students, in later years, have in turn been an encouragement to me! I am also grateful for the close friendships I enjoy with others who are mature in their own faith, providing a context for mutual strengthening and encouragement.

*Two are better than one, because they have a good return for their work: If one falls down, his friend can lift him up. But pity the man who falls and has no one to help him up (Ecclesiastes 4:9, 10).*

*Praise be to the God and Father of our Lord Jesus Christ, the Father of compassion and the God of all comfort, who comforts us in all our troubles, so that we can comfort those in any trouble with the comfort we ourselves receive from God (2 Corinthians 1:3, 4).*

As we encourage and support one another along the way, and share the journey together, our love for God and one another grows deeper, and spills over to in turn embrace others who are broken and hurting – so that through our redeemed, healed and restored lives, others too can walk trash free! It is said that hurt people, hurt people. But it is also true that healed people, heal people – especially when that healing originates with the One who's great Name is Healer!

## What About You?

1. In what ways do you feel trapped into a life of the "walking wounded" rather than living out your life from a place of healing and restoration?

2. Consider praying this prayer, and then proactively seeking out a trusted, mature believer to come alongside to strengthen and help you: "Lord, I realize that I cannot do this alone. I want to walk in wholeness, and for that I need both Your power, and the help of fellow believers. Please lead me to a resource person who can help me to live out my life as a new creation in You."

# CHAPTER 13
# FREELY RECEIVED, FREELY GIVE

*I*n Luke chapter 7, we encounter a woman who pours out an extravagant expression of love at the feet of Jesus. This event occurs in the home of Simon the Pharisee, who is hosting Jesus at the time. While Simon does not give voice to His disapproval, he sneers to himself, "If this man were a prophet, he would know who is touching him and what kind of a woman she is – that she is a sinner."

She was unclean, and to be despised and avoided. That is all Simon could perceive of the woman.

Not surprisingly, Jesus sees the woman differently. To Simon's chagrin, Jesus has also heard Simon's thoughts as clearly as if he had spoken them aloud. The Teacher/Redeemer proceeds to tell Simon a story that makes an unavoidable point: that those who have been forgiven much, in turn love much. Love who? Love both the Lord and others much! The woman's extravagant love flows from her gratitude for the abundant grace of forgiveness poured out into her life.

Simon could hardly miss the dual point that Jesus was making: Simon, who had made it clear that he loved little – not even showing his invited guest the most basic respect and hospitality; Simon, who is full of his own self-righteousness; this Simon is himself in need of a great deal of forgiveness. Yet he is so full of self-righteous pride that he is blind to and oblivious of his own need for repentance. The result is a spiritual and emotional poverty that renders love for Jesus or anyone else stone cold. He has failed to perceive his own deep need for forgiveness – and can therefore neither extend mercy to this woman, nor comprehend the depths of her love.

The writer of Hebrews tells us to *throw off everything that hinders* in the "race" set before us (Hebrews 12:1). There are many things that have the potential of hindering us in this "race". Yet in ministering to people, there is one issue that seems to be a major stumbling block for many: that of forgiveness of others who have wounded them.

This is not a matter to be treated lightly or superficially. I am deeply aware that many have suffered grievously at the hands of those who have acted heinously and have caused deep and lasting damage and destruction. And yet... what does the Bible say about this?

Firstly, it tells us that we are to be mindful of how much we ourselves have been forgiven by God. Every one of us falls so far short of His perfect holiness, that He cannot even abide our filth in His presence. The Bible tells us that even when we consider ourselves to be "righteous" in our conduct, in God's eyes our so-called righteousness looks no better than "filthy rags" (Isaiah 64:6).

In the twenty-first century we have lost sight of what was meant by the "filthy rags" at the time that these words were written. In its historical and cultural context, "filthy rags" refer to a woman's discarded menstrual cloths – regarded in that culture at that time as the filthiest object of all. And the Bible tells us this is how God views what we perceive as our "righteousness"! Yet He forgave us freely in spite of how offensive our filth is to His holiness, and in His love and grace, He instead clothes us in the radiant purity of His own Son, so that we can draw near to Him. Our response to this overwhelming love and mercy can only be to pour out our own love at His feet.

Secondly, our attitude to others, no matter what they have done or how grievously they have hurt us, is to allow this same love of God in Christ Jesus, to flow out of our own lives to them. Given what we may have suffered at the hands of others, we balk at this. In doing so, we may be operating under a couple of misconceptions:

1. We feel that forgiving another means that they get off scot-free – and we want them to be held accountable for what they have done. Yet the Bible teaches that it is when we forgive, and release that person to the Lord, that we relinquish them to Him to deal with. Doing so is a measure of our trust in God – that He will do exactly what is needed, according to His knowledge, wisdom and power, which are far greater than ours. *Will not the judge of all the earth do right? (Genesis 18:25).*

   Very importantly, forgiving others releases **us** from bondage. For as long as we hold unforgiveness and bitterness in our hearts towards another, we remain chained to them and to the woundedness they caused. Choosing to forgive, by an act of our will, severs that chain. God desires our freedom – and it is for our own benefit that He requires of us that we forgive. Indeed, He goes so far as to say that we will be forgiven to the extent that we extend forgiveness to others! *And when you stand praying, if you hold anything against anyone, forgive him, so that your Father in heaven may forgive you your sins (Mark 11:25).*

2. We confuse forgiveness with trust. Forgiveness is freely given out of our love for the Lord and our thankfulness for His forgiveness towards us. Trust, however, is earned. We can forgive others freely, thereby releasing them to the Lord, and freeing ourselves from bondage to them and their actions. However, restored trust requires a change in behavior in the other person that remains consistent over time. This may involve a long process. A Biblical example of this is Zacchaeus' transformed behavior after his encounter with Jesus. He not only stopped skimming money for himself from the taxes he collected, but he returned the money he had already accumulated in this devious way. Another example is Saul, the persecutor and killer of Christians. After his encounter with the risen Lord, it took some time before the believers were willing to trust him. This happened only as he consistently lived out his transformed life.

I am convinced that unforgiveness is the most significant hindrance to wholeness and heart healing. We need to stay clear of assuming a stance that others have to earn or ask for our forgiveness before we are willing to give it. Jesus not only taught otherwise, but He demonstrated it in and through His own life. We often talk about the love that sent Jesus to the cross: His passion for humanity, demonstrated in the sacrifice of Himself, so that you and I could be reconciled in our relationship with God.

But how often have we considered what that love looked like at the rock face in the life of Jesus, incarnate in human flesh, experiencing all the joys and sorrows of the human condition?

As Son of Man, He poured Himself out into the lives of others constantly:

He poured new hope into ravaged hearts;

He poured new healing into deep woundedness;

He poured forgiveness into guilt-ridden spirits;

He poured new life into blighted lives;

He poured new love into those who knew rejection and abandonment;

He poured time and attention into those who were lost and hurting;

He poured Himself out in healing and redemption and restoration and care and authentic relationship, touching lives with the riches of the Kingdom of God, giving of Himself tirelessly and constantly.

And after He had done all of this:

The mob screamed, "Crucify Him!"

His closest companions deserted Him.

His onlookers mocked Him.

His enemies reviled Him and spat on Him.

His leaders subjected Him to hours of torture followed by a long and excruciating death.

And then at the hour of His greatest suffering... the Father turned away as Jesus took upon Himself all of humanity's filthy sin.

The words that Jesus spoke during the time of His arrest, trials and crucifixion resound through redemption history. Yet the words He did **not** speak may be just as significant:

"After all I've done for you..."

These are the words He never said.

Instead He said, "Father forgive them..."

In one sentence, Jesus demonstrated what it is to forgive freely, in the midst of pain, and when the perpetrators of that pain neither deserved nor asked for that forgiveness.

God's working in human lives is always for redemption: ours and that of others. For the sake of our own freedom, our own wholeness, He requires of us that we forgive – and then trust Him with the results. Forgiveness is not a feeling: it is a choice, a decision made in obedience to the Lord you love. Once you make that choice, the feelings of hurt and betrayal may not immediately change. But over time your feelings will begin to transform and come into alignment with the choice you have made.

Unforgiveness provides the soil for bitterness to grow. It poisons our lives and relationships and the people around us. Forgiveness provides the soil for healing and joy to grow, and releases the grace of God to permeate our lives and relationships.

Only in this way can we truly sever our bondage to the broken past for once and for all, thereby leaving room for the fullness of God's redemption to bear fruit.

*See to it that no one falls short of the grace of God and that no bitter root grows up to cause trouble and defile many (Hebrews 12:15).*

When we choose to forgive, the "trash" of bitterness is transformed into the radiance of God's glory emanating from our lives, and the sweetness of His fragrance permeating the atmosphere.

---

### <u>What About You?</u>

1. What are the names of the people from whom you have withheld forgiveness? Are you willing to choose to forgive them before the Lord, out of love for Him and obedience to His Word?

2. Pray: "Lord, thank You for Your grace poured out into my life, in love and forgiveness. My love response to Your love, is to choose, right now, to forgive _____ (insert names here). I do so in obedience to Your Word, trusting You with all the circumstances and experiences and outcomes. I ask You now that as I choose to walk in forgiveness, Your Holy Spirit will have free access to my heart, to heal and transform it, causing my feelings to come into alignment with You and with Your Word."

---

# CHAPTER 14
## WHEN THE ROAD LEADS THROUGH THE WILDERNESS

*C*radled between the sea and the mountains on the south western coast of South Africa, nestles the exquisite city of Cape Town. Almost a thousand miles away, in the north interior, sprawls the vibrant highland city of Johannesburg. Spanning much of the distance between these two cities, a vast plateau known as the Great Karoo stretches and yawns like a tawny African lion. This semi-arid plain both seduces and challenges the eye with its limitlessness – a monotonous terrain broken sporadically by dramatic rock formations and outcrops scattered as randomly as if a giant fist had flung them there. Its shimmering summer heat is alleviated only occasionally by the high drama of thunderstorms spectacular in their power-and-light displays. Its early winter mornings are achingly cold, freezing the dry ground as hard as granite.

Population is sparse: sprawling sheep farms straddle the expanses between quaint farming towns and villages a hundred miles or more apart. The road that runs through the Great Karoo is long and flat. On each side of the highway, stones and boulders strewn across the scrubby terrain are barely distinguishable from the dust-coated sheep that graze there. Far-flung farmhouses are sheltered among man-made oases of pepper and cypress trees.

Traffic accidents along this road are frequent, mostly because travelers drive at high speed, motivated both by the irresistibly straight road intersected only by an elusive horizon, and by the desire to leave the semi-arid terrain behind them as fast as possible. To many the Karoo is territory to negotiate as a matter of necessity on the way to somewhere else; it is not a region to linger in.

I drove the 1400 kilometer (about 900 miles) distance between Cape Town and Johannesburg on a number of occasions. When I lived in Cape Town, I occasionally drove to Johannesburg to visit family there; and later, when I lived in Johannesburg, I drove to Cape Town at least once a year to vacation in that breathtaking tourist trap.

Sometimes I made the trip in a day — approximately fourteen hours of driving, including a stop every three hours to stretch my legs. On other occasions I stopped overnight, in either Colesburg or Beaufort West — Karoo towns that lie about 300 kilometers (or 200 miles) apart. But whether I did the trip in a day or in two days, I never felt inclined to race through the Karoo as if it was an unavoidable and unpleasant experience best dispatched with.

I love the Karoo. Its colors and hues shift constantly with the traversing sun, in changes both subtle and mesmerizing. Dawn and dusk splash splendor at once exhilarating and soothing across a horizon seamed to infinity. At night, far from the incessant clamor of intrusive city lights, the black velvet canopy forms a bottomless backdrop to the star-struck pageantry of nature's own planetarium. It is as if nature pulls out all her stops in the Great Karoo. To me the Great Karoo is just that – great.

So it was that on a trip home from Johannesburg to Cape Town one summer's evening, I decided to pull over in Colesburg for the night, and continue my journey in the morning. That way I could savor the Karoo just a little longer. The next morning I left Colesburg shortly after 5:30 a.m. Dawn's palette was sweeping the sky in flamboyant brushstrokes, and the day seemed poised to bestow a joyful benediction. For the next hour I reveled in the view coming at me through my car windscreen, marveling at the God who had made it all.

It was after this first hour of travel that the realization stole over me that I recognized neither the road I was on, nor the surroundings I was in. The gradual panning and merging of the terrain had been so subtle that I was nonplussed to find myself in completely unfamiliar territory. Where was I? Peace swiftly turned to anxiety as I peered ahead, willing a sign, any sign to come into view. Finally one did: one that said "Middelburg 50 kilometers" (about 31 miles). Middelburg! Middelburg is in the Eastern Cape! I was headed in the wrong direction altogether! How had that happened?

It took some moments for perplexity to turn to comprehension regarding how and where I had gone wrong – moments during which I continued barreling towards an unplanned destination. From Colesburg the road divides into two separate highways, leading in different directions – the N1 to Cape Town in the southwest, and the N9 that ultimately, through ways winding, devious, and inter-connected, culminates in the eastern seaboard cities of Port Elizabeth and East London. Entranced by dawn in the semi-wilderness, I had been careering blithely down the wrong road!

Fortunately, albeit at the cost of a significant detour, I eventually came across a turnoff onto a much smaller road that, cutting through endless farmland, eventually triangulates back to the N1. What a relief to be able to correct my course! However, by this time I was no longer relaxed, since I was now driving with my gas tank showing "empty". I had failed to fill the gas tank in Colesburg, thinking that I could easily make Beaufort West before needing to do so. Now as the miles inched away beneath the wheels like a treadmill on slow speed, I kept willing my car on, praying for an elusive gas station. Eventually a lone gas pump beckoned in the distance. Could it be a mirage, shimmering in the heat? But no – it was real – I had reached the tiny farm hamlet of Hanover.

Hanover is an historical village quaintly stuck in the 19th century. It was once the home of Olive Schreiner, famous South African writer, women's activist, and author of the classic "The Story of an African Farm". Unfortunately, on this occasion I was in no mind to appreciate either Hanover's picturesque character or its historical significance. The only gas pump for miles around was the single-minded focus of my attention. I had been imagining having to abandon my car on the side of the road, in order to tramp who knows how far across expansive farmland to the nearest farmhouse to ask for assistance – "nearest" being a highly relative concept in the middle of the Karoo!

The experience has remained memorable – not because I took the wrong road, but because I was so entranced by this semi-arid region, that I became oblivious to what direction I was traveling in. There is a lesson in that, but the point here is that while many others approached that semi-wilderness as a place to hasten in and out of as fast as possible, I saw the beauty, the blessing, the majesty of the wilderness – and not only embraced it, but reveled in it.

It is not only the collected trash of our lives that we trip over. We also all stumble through wilderness experiences at times, unsure how to negotiate such rocky terrain. Human nature being what it is, most often our reaction to personal wilderness experiences is to get out of the wasteland as fast as we can. In the interim, feeling ill-equipped to negotiate such inhospitable landscape, we often cry and complain about the terrible and difficult place we are in, convinced that life surely has something much better – and better deserved – than this seemingly hostile desert place. Or perhaps we become weary and discouraged and give up altogether. Either way, we regard the wilderness, both as a place and an experience, with aversion. It sears us with its heat, it numbs us with its cold, its impenetrable darkness fills us with unnamed fears; we feel starved in its sparseness, and alienated by its starkness; we are left lost in its emptiness and bereft in its barrenness; we are parched by its dryness, wearied by its monotony and paralyzed by the fury of its sudden storms breaking over our heads.

Yet… in our haste to abandon the wilderness, is it possible that we might be overlooking the splendor and abundance that are to be found there? Splendor? Abundance? These are hardly attributes we expect of a wilderness! Feeling alone and exposed, we rush to find something, anything that seems to hold the promise of safer shelter, greater fruitfulness, more hope, better succor than this desert place. And in our headlong panic to get out of this wasteland, we fail to see what it has to offer: not only its treasures, its beauty, its majesty, but also its purpose, peace, and joy.

The Great Karoo offers not only surface beauty to those who will slow down long enough to have their eyes opened to the experience. Deep in its seared soil lies hidden treasure: diamonds forged through heat and pressure; gold clasped in fists of rock.

What if...? What if there are treasures yet waiting to be discovered, buried in the landscape of our personal wilderness experiences? What if self-pity blinds us to what awaits delightful discovery there; what if in our haste to leave such seemingly hostile experiences behind, we rush by something of inestimable worth? Where do we look to find such things in our personal "dry and weary land"? Or rather, **how** do we look? For what is needed to discover the riches of the wilderness is a new way of seeing.

There is no better way of seeing than through heaven's prism. The Bible sparkles with the wealth of both the pasture and the wilderness; both the mountaintop and the plateau; both the oasis and the desert expanse; both the meadow and the wasteland. When we are willing to take the hand of God and allow Him to lead us through the wilderness; to reveal to us its directional clues; to teach us to view its landscape through His eyes, it is then that our hearts begin to open to a secret beauty that can be discovered nowhere else – and we will never be the same again. Rather than crying out for the wilderness to be changed, we instead find ourselves eternally transformed by it.

The wasteland experience need not be wasted. However, to discover its worth we need to give it not merely a fleeing glance, but our receptive awareness and attention. Come, take His hand with me, and let us dare to journey there together: Not hastening through with protesting cry, but instead soaking up its stillness, and lingering to look and listen, and if necessary, dig deep to find the treasures that will fill our hearts with unsurpassed wonder.

In Hosea 2:14, 15, God speaks these wonderful words of promise: *"... I will lead her into the wilderness and speak tenderly to her. There I will give her back her vineyards, and will make the Valley of Achor a door of hope."*

Here God makes several interconnected statements and promises:

1. There are times when the wilderness we experience is the wilderness He has **led** us into. This was true of the Israelites in the Old Testament, and it is often true of our own lives. Instead of frantically trying to find our way back out of the wilderness, perhaps we need to be still enough to hear and discover the purpose for which God has led us there. For we are not alone in the wilderness – God too, is there.

2. It is in the wilderness place that He wants to "speak tenderly" to us. Perhaps the wilderness is the only place emptied enough of the "noise" of life, for us to be able to finally hear His voice! Perhaps it takes being in a wilderness place before we finally turn to hear what it is He has to say, instead of running after every other "voice" that calls to us. When we stop long enough to listen, what we will hear will be His voice of tenderness and love washing our hearts with His healing words, and speaking fresh purpose into our lives.

3. As a result of the wilderness experience, He will cause increased fruitfulness to be restored in and through our lives. He will sovereignly take what seems like our most barren places and experiences, and transform them by His power, into our life's greatest fruitfulness.

4. "Achor" means "trouble". The very experiences that have seemed like the deepest trouble in our lives, God will cause to become the doorway to the most delightful hope.

All of this comes only in and resulting from, our wilderness experiences! Let us therefore not fight to get out of the wilderness; let us rather open our ears, our eyes, our hearts to discover what treasures are to be found there.

In the book of Hosea, God likens His people to a wanton woman who is determined to go her own willful way. In the verses mentioned above, He says that He will use the wilderness experience not as punishment, but to woo His people back to Himself.

God uses **our** wilderness experiences also, to woo us back to Himself, to speak His tender words of love to us. As we respond to His wooing in that desert place, instead of experiencing barrenness, He brings forth fruitfulness from our lives – in the wilderness! In His great love, God turns the place of trouble in our lives into hope-filled opportunity. And in the middle of this wilderness, our hearts burst with a joy that overflows into the sound of our rejoicing ringing across the expanse of a wasteland redeemed by the Lover of our souls!

God picks up this theme of His particular, tender care of us in the wilderness, in the book of Revelation. Here again we meet a woman who represents His people. However, this time the woman ends up in the wilderness not because of her own willful ways, but because of the attempted attack of the enemy against her. The first time this happens, the woman flees into the wilderness, to *a place prepared for her by God* (Revelation 12:6). It is in this wilderness that she is protected and cared for, for an extended period.

Later, the enemy comes after her a second time. This time, *The woman was given the two wings of a great eagle, so that she might fly to the place prepared for her in the desert, where she would be taken care of… out of the serpent's reach (Revelation 12:14).*

If you are in a wilderness place right now, rather than bewailing your circumstances, stop awhile and look around you. Could it be that you are in the very place of God's tender care, provision and protection that He has prepared for you? Could it be that in this place He is wooing you to learn dependence on and surrender to His love and purposes? Could it be that the place that seems so barren is the very place of sovereign fruitfulness?

Perhaps He has brought you to a place not dense with dry dust, but bursting with unspeakable treasure. The wilderness can be bewildering to us. But God knows every part of it intimately; Jesus experienced it personally, in the flesh. The only way to see the wilderness is through His eyes; the only way to negotiate the wilderness, is to follow Him:

> *My Lord knows the way through the wilderness*
> *All I have to do is follow*
> *Strength for today is mine all the way*
> *And all I need for tomorrow*
> *My Lord knows the way through the wilderness*
> *All I have to do is follow*[12].

[12]  My Lord Knows the Way: Sydney E. Cox

### What About You?

1. Does it feel as if you are in a wilderness right now? Rather than trying to escape the barrenness of the wilderness, are you willing to find what treasures the Lord might have for you there?

2. Pray: "Lord, instead of trying to get out of this place I find myself in, I want to become still so that I can hear Your voice. Would You 'speak tenderly' to me here, show me what treasures You have for me here, and cause this very time and place in my life to be the gateway to my life's greatest fruitfulness and hope."

# CHAPTER 15
# THE WONDERS OF
# THE WILDERNESS

*I* loved physical activity: hiking, running, swimming, playing field hockey, climbing trees and launching myself out into clear air to land like a cat on the ground before climbing back up for more, jumping on a trampoline...

It was on a trampoline that I first tore the ligaments in my ankle. Shooting high into the sky was exhilarating – but then I lost my balance in the air, came down awkwardly with my foot folded beneath me, and spent the next six weeks in a plaster cast.

In the ten years that followed, I injured that ankle repeatedly, until the ligaments were almost completely torn away. Surgeons decided to do a tendon graft, pinning another tendon from my leg onto my ankle, and securing it there with a titanium pin. I spent several days in hospital after the surgery, and was then sent home. Three days later, my mother came home from work to find me unconscious. A frantic race to the hospital brought bad news: I had septicemia that had already reached my brain. My family was told to prepare themselves for my possible death – and that even if I did survive, there was a strong possibility that my leg would have to be amputated and/or I would be left with brain damage.

I was 21 years old.

I was pumped full of intravenous antibiotics, and had 24/7 nursing care. My family and our church went to prayer. My life was spared, my leg was saved... my sisters say that the verdict is still out on the brain damage part!

The worst seemed to be over, but I was not through my personal wilderness yet – not by a long way. During the eighteen months that followed, I had constant infection inside the surgery site, had to undergo further surgery every six to eight weeks, lived on massive doses of antibiotics, and was unable to walk. Nevertheless, being determined to remain as fit as possible, I continued to find ways to exercise – including going for long walks on my crutches, forming first blisters, then calluses on my hands.

Finally a new surgeon and a new hospital discovered the source of the trouble: a piece of tendon that had been cut off during the first surgery had been left inside the wound, and had been rotting away inside of me all this time. It was a miracle that I did not lose my leg from the resulting infection!

For several weeks after the final surgery that resolved this issue, I felt wonderful: my body felt tangibly different once the necrotic material had been removed. Then, about three months after this last surgery, I started contracting antibiotic-resistant bronchial and urinary tract infections. By this time my family had relocated to another city, and I had decided not to accompany them. I was working full-time to support myself, and studying at night to complete my university degree with a triple major. With constant illness dogging my every step, including a bout of mononucleosis, it became more and more difficult to keep going. I felt caught in an endless wilderness of debilitating exhaustion with no possibility of relief or release. There were days when I thought that dying would have been the easier option.

Nevertheless, keep going I did, and after completing graduate work in the field of Education, I began a teaching career at the age of 29. As much as I loved my job, the recurring infections continued to drag at me. In spite of this, however, I took up long-distance cycling, and competed in several races, including the world-renowned Cape Argus Cycle Tour. Then, coming into my second year of participating in this race, on my final training ride, I was hit by a hit-and-run driver in a van.

Once more my life was spared: I was flung into the air, and came down head first, landing partly on my face, partly on my helmet, in the middle of the road. A passing jogger dragged me out of the middle of the road before I got run over by oncoming traffic. My bicycle was trashed, and my face smashed. Two black eyes, a split lip, broken teeth, a fractured bone in my leg, and internal bruising later, I was in no state to ride in any race!

Flesh finally knit back together, bones and bruises healed, and yet more antibiotics staved off any infection. I took up running instead. A year later, I was bitten by a tick, and contracted tick bite fever – requiring more antibiotics.

In addition, kidney and bronchial infections persisted, with multiple courses of various antibiotics required for each round. By this time, this pattern had kept repeating for ten years. Finally I looked up my childhood family physician – a big teddy-bear of a man full of compassion, who was like a father. I burst into tears and cried on his shoulder! It did not take him long to ascertain that my immune system had been significantly compromised by the original surgeries and ongoing infections, and the continuous, large doses of antibiotics.

It took several more years to arrive at an effective means of redressing my compromised immunity, and to learn how to "manage" it. In the meantime, I kept teaching and studying, and also began writing, in spite of periodically hitting the wall and having to take three months off at a time, to recover.

The single event of that first surgery – which should have been a straightforward procedure with a six-week recovery time – propelled me into a personal wilderness that impacted the remainder of my entire adult life. I eventually came to the end of myself, and there came a day when I sat in a church service, too weak to even stand for worship, and I said to the Lord, "I'm done. I'm no use to myself, I'm no use to anyone else, and I'm no use to You." I had just turned forty.

That day the pastor preached from one of the texts that I had responded to as a twelve-year-old, as God's call on my life: *And He died for all, that those who live should no longer live for themselves but for Him who died for them and was raised again… All this is from God, who reconciled us to Himself through Christ and gave us the ministry of reconciliation: that God was reconciling the world to Himself in Christ, not counting men's sins against them. And He has committed to us the message of reconciliation. We are therefore Christ's ambassadors, as though God were making His appeal through us (2 Corinthians 5:15 – 20).*

In spite of the obstacles, I had always been fiercely independent and determinedly ambitious. I did not easily accept closed doors or anything else that stood in my way. If I only tried hard enough, long enough, was my attitude, I could accomplish anything. If obstacles obstructed my pursuit, I would find a way to get around them, tunnel under them, climb over them, or bash them down.

*…He died for all, that those who live should no longer live for themselves but for Him who died for them…*

I had always loved the Lord. My life as a teacher was one of constant ministry into the lives of others. But… I was living to fulfill my own goals and ambitions.

It took a long journey through the wilderness to teach me two things: Complete dependence on God and not on myself; abandoned surrender to Him and His calling and purpose.

There had been times along the way when I had asked, "why me?" Why should I, of all people, I who loved physical activity, be afflicted with an uncooperative immune system that left me with lowered stamina? At one point I felt that it had ruined my life.

But no longer do I feel that way. In fact, now I am grateful for a God who is gracious and caring enough, a God who cares so deeply about **His** purposes for and in my life, that He allowed me to experience the wilderness so that I could learn how to place my dependence in Him and not myself. A God whose purposes are such valuable treasure, that He takes the time and trouble to form them in the wilderness.

I came to see life's wilderness in a new way: not as a place to be shunned at all costs, but as place of God's most loving provision. Very often it is in the wilderness that we learn to flourish!

How can this be? An illustration can be found in nature in the Northern Cape region of South Africa called the Namaqualand. The Namaqualand too, is a semi-arid place with topography that transitions from scrubby terrain to giant sand dunes in the west as the traveler draws nearer to the Atlantic coast. Summer days are heart-pounding hot; and winter nights are brain-freeze cold. Most of the year nothing but a few straggling drought-resistant plants survive there.

It is in winter that just a small amount of rainfall descends over the Namaqualand. Less than two months later in early spring, the land is carpeted with wild flowers in whites and yellows and oranges and purples and pinks in every direction as far as the eye can see. Tourists come from all over the country and the world to see this phenomenon.

All through the long, dry, arid months, little seeds lie under the seared soil of the Namaqualand, waiting for that little bit of water that coaxes life from those shriveled seeds. Small roots begin to probe downward; bright shoots begin to push upward toward the light, and then the desert bursts into bloom!

This reminds me of a promise given in Isaiah 35: *The desert and the parched land will be glad; the wilderness will rejoice and blossom. Like the crocus, it will burst into bloom; it will rejoice greatly and shout for joy... Strengthen the feeble hands, steady the knees that give way; say to those with fearful hearts, "Be strong, do not fear; your God will* come..." ... *the redeemed will walk there... Gladness and joy will overtake them, and sorrow and sighing will flee away.*

What wilderness place do you find yourself in? Isn't it true that our personal wilderness experiences sap our strength? Our reflex reaction again, is to cry and plead to be delivered out of the wilderness.

But God's promise is that instead, He will **transform** the wilderness, and in the process, also transforms you and I! We may well feel dried out and shriveled up and without hope or strength in our season of barrenness. But the Living Water promises His refreshing rain to restore life to our seared souls, and soon the landscape of our lives will flourish and bloom with the presence and purposes of God and delight will abound!

I am forever thankful that my personal wilderness experiences turned me away from pursuing empty ambition, to instead allowing the Living Water to fill my life until it overflows with His glorious purpose. How magnificently more satisfying than my desperate attempts to escape my wilderness!

While David was in the Desert of Judah, he wrote these words in Psalm 63:1: *You, God, are my God, earnestly I seek You; I thirst for You, my whole being longs for You, in a dry and parched land where there is no water.*

When the barrenness of the wilderness compels us to seek God Himself, we too will discover what David went on to articulate in verse 3: *Because Your love is better than life, my lips will glorify You.*

Your wilderness too, can be transformed to a place filled with wonder and beauty as the God of glory redeems the scorched and dry places, sending heaven's refreshing rain to bring forth life from barren places: A place drenched in His inexhaustible love.

### Sower of the Seed

In a landscape once laid waste
By trampled trust —
Lying fallow, and fortified
Against all who
Trespass —
A single, hesitant shoot
Peeps unexpected
From charred soil, lifting tentative
Tendrils towards the Son's
Embrace.

Oh Sower of the seed, whose scarred
And tender hands
Caressed this once discarded
Kernel to life
Unseen,
Now shelter, nourish, nurture it,
'Til desolated
Fields spill flowering fragrance
Over fruitful land
Redeemed.

Avril VanderMerwe © 2005

<u>**What About You?**</u>

1. Do you feel like that little dried out seed, lying under the burning sands of your personal desert place?

2. Pray: "Lord I need You, Living Water, to drench my personal barrenness with the refreshing rain of Your presence, power, and purposes. As I wait on You, would You fill me once again, and bring forth new life in every scorched and dry place and circumstance, and cause me to overflow with the beauty of Your fruitfulness."

# CHAPTER 16
# DESIGNED TO SHINE

*G*old. South Africa leads the world in gold mining, and has the richest gold deposits in the world. Far removed from the glittering splendor of golden jewelry and coins on dazzling display in upmarket boutiques, mine workers labor and sweat in tunnels deep under the earth of southern Africa, extracting the precious metal that drives much of the world's economy.

When I was growing up, tourists brave enough to do so, could take a tour of a gold mine in South Africa. This is what they experienced:

The first step involves riding a skiff down a shaft that plunges an average of 2800 to 3400 meters below the surface (9,186 – 11,150 feet) before alighting in a tunnel where, at that depth, the heat is so intense that it is unbearable to human beings. Air conditioning is piped into these tunnels, to keep miners safe.

It is in the tunnels that rock is blasted with explosives, and drilled with high-power drills, and hammered with mallets and chisels, to extract those parts of the rock that bear the gold. This gold-bearing rock is then crushed and sifted to separate as much of the gold from the rock as possible. Finally, the visitor can watch as the gold is fired at a temperature of 1947.52 degrees Fahrenheit to purify it. The sight of pure, liquid gold being poured as it comes through this refining process, is dazzling to behold.

This pure liquid gold is then poured into large brick molds, where it cools and solidifies. The visitor's final experience is to sit in a room facing a table draped with a velvet cloth. Here it is that a mine official displays a cooled brick of gold, handled by gloved hands, and has it placed before the audience, on the table. He then issues a challenge: "If one of the strongest men in the room can come and pick up this brick of gold with one hand, you can take it home with you."

What an opportunity! Of course the mining official knows that there is no risk of losing the bar of gold to any would-be strongman, because that gold, having gone through all the harshness of the purification process, is so weighty (about 500 lbs) that nobody can pick up the gold brick with one hand.

Can you imagine if gold-bearing rock could talk? Would it not cry out in agony at all the blasting, drilling, hammering, crushing, sifting, fiery experiences it had to go through? And yet the end result of all of that trauma, is pure gold of inestimable worth, carrying great weight.

In his second letter to the Corinthians, in chapter 4 verse 17, the apostle Paul writes these words: *For our light and momentary troubles are achieving for us an eternal glory that far **outweighs** them all.*

The glory achieved in our lives through what seems like a harsh and agonizing refining process, far outweighs the troubles we experience!

"But ah!" you cry, "You don't understand! My troubles are not 'light and momentary' at all! They are grievous and overwhelming and have gone on so long that I just can't take it anymore!"

In terms of real human experience, Paul's troubles were not "light and momentary" either. If you put together all that he suffered throughout his life's ministry, you discover that he went through more trouble, pain, and suffering than most people experience in a lifetime. And yet, because of the great weight and value of God's glory in Paul that was forged in him through those very troubles, he came to view those troubles as trivial compared to the glory that resulted.

God does not **send** trouble to us, but He sometimes **allows** trouble to intersect our lives. Like the gold mining and purification process, that trouble can feel as if a destructive explosion has rocked our world. It can feel as if we are being drilled by hardship, and relentlessly hammered and brutally crushed by problems and difficulties and sorrows, and sifted by shaking. It can feel as if the heat has been turned up in our lives to unbearable intensity until we feel as if our hearts and bones have been melted down and poured out.

You may feel like David felt as expressed in Psalm 22: *I am poured out like water, and all my bones are out of joint. My heart has turned to wax; it has melted within me.*

When this happens, we have a choice. Even as we cry out to the One who Paul calls in chapter 1 of 2 Corinthians the *Father of compassion*, we can simultaneously ask Him to produce His great weight of glory in us through the very troubles and trials we are experiencing.

You can see this very process in Psalm 22, when, after crying out his agony to the Lord, David ends his psalm with victory and praise in the God who redeems all things.

In the midst of all his grief and loss, Job too, understood this, and declared, *"But He knows the way that I take; when He has tested me, I will come forth as gold."*

Rather than our troubles producing in us the dross or the "trash" of resentment and bitterness and doubt and despair, they can instead cause us to bear within ourselves the weight and the eternal value of God's radiant glory. When gold goes through the refining process, the dross is removed, revealing and releasing the "glory" of the pure gold.

How, practically, does this happen?

First of all, as mentioned previously, and as exemplified by King David, pour out your grief, confusion, and pain to the Lord. He is a safe recipient of all our anguish.

Secondly, surrender and entrust yourself to the Lord in the midst of whatever painful process you are enduring. Ask Him to take away any "dross" there may be in your heart or thinking or attitude, and to purify your heart with the help of the Holy Spirit. Thank Him for the Holy Spirit who is your Comforter and Counselor always, and for the Word of God that dwells in you richly, and is living and powerful.

Thirdly, we are **designed** to shine! The book of Hebrews says this of Jesus: *He is the radiance of the Father's glory and the exact representation of His being.*

Have you ever wondered what God is like? Look at Jesus! Look at His life, His character; hear His words; witness His heart of love expressed through the way He engaged with people; see His power manifest in all He said and did. Jesus **is** the exact expression of the glory, majesty, love and radiance of God Himself.

In fact, as mentioned previously, Jesus said of Himself, *"Anyone who has seen Me, has seen the Father" (John 14:9)*. His name is Immanuel which means "God with us"!

The Bible exhorts us to *fix our eyes on Jesus, the author and perfecter of our faith… (Hebrews 12:2)*. Not only does He perfect our faith, but when we make Him who is "the radiance of the Father's glory" the focus of our attention, something amazing begins to happen in us. This is described in 2 Corinthians 3:18: *And we, who with unveiled faces all reflect the Lord's glory, are being transformed into His likeness with ever-increasing glory, which comes from the Lord, who is the Spirit.*

Our thoughts, our emotions, our relationships, our lives reflect whatever occupies and dominates our attention. And when Jesus is the One who has captured our hearts, and is the One who holds our gaze, and dominates our attention, our lives begin to reflect **Him** and His radiance!

The Victorian Scottish writer, Thomas Carlyle, once said that people become like the gods they serve. Whatever or whoever predominates in our lives and dominates our attention and consumes our thoughts and captures our emotions, is what or who is going to be reflected in and through our lives. In our words and conduct, we begin to mirror that person or thing. In making Jesus the One upon whom our attention, thoughts and desires are centered, we have the opportunity to reflect Him who is *the radiance of the Father's glory*.

What does "unveiled faces" mean? It simply means that we open our hearts completely to allow Jesus to reveal Himself to us, and pour His love into the depths of our beings - not "veiling" our innermost selves in a way that denies Him access. And then, with those same open hearts, we turn and engage with others around us, allowing the glory of who He is and His love, to spill from our lives.

We are a people marked by love: The consuming, extravagant love of God lavishly poured out. His love has an amazing effect on our hearts: it causes them to both fill and expand, increasing our capacity for yet more of His love. The more we look to Jesus, the more He fills our hearts; the more He fills them, the more He increases their capacity to both contain and give more and more of His love to others.

Psalm 34:5 tells us: *Those who look to Him are **radiant**; their faces are never covered with shame.* Recently I had a conversation with someone who I know has been through tremendous difficulty for many years. I had not seen her in a while, and when I asked how she was doing, with tears in her eyes, she said, "I feel so incredibly blessed. I have been overwhelmed by the love of God, and I have realized it's not about how much I love Him - it's all about how much He loves me! And realizing this has enabled me to let go and stop trying to be in control, because I can rest in the knowledge that in His great love for me, He will cause all things to work for my good." In spite of the problems, she was radiant with the love of the Lord, and no longer the downcast and tormented person I met a few years ago!

Can you allow your heart too, to gaze upon His radiance? Let the barriers down, and open your heart to receive the love He yearns to pour out into you. The result will be a heart and life transformed by the experience! A heart that continues to hunger for more and more of this One who is the *radiance of the Father's glory*. And before you know it, your life too, will begin to reflect His radiance for others to see. You might remain oblivious to your own radiance, because your attention is not on yourself, but on the Lover of your soul. But others will see it… and begin to want what you have… and it will draw them to seek the same transformational Love…

*For it is the God who commanded light to shine out of darkness, who has shone in our hearts to give the light of the knowledge of the glory of God in the face of Jesus Christ (2 Corinthians 4:6 NKJV).*

---

### What About You?

1.  Have you felt as if trouble, hardship and heartache have blasted and crushed and burned your life, leaving you feeling beaten up and expended?

2.  Set aside as much time as necessary to pour your heart out to the One who is "the Father of all compassion". Then invite Him to forge in you, through these very circumstances, the weight of His glory. Begin to choose daily, moment by moment, to focus your attention on Him, keeping your eyes riveted on His, and opening your heart to allow all that He is to flood your being until it radiates with the light of Jesus Christ.

# CHAPTER 17
# GENERATIONAL BLESSING

"*D*o you think I'm cursed?"

This is a question I am asked from time to time, by people who have experienced multiplied troubles and tragedies in their own lives, and often also in the lives of immediate and extended family members.

It is a question that has been raised even in my own extended family:

Many years ago, among the rough and tumble of the early twentieth-century South African gold fields, hundreds of workers had been brought to South Africa from China, to help work in the gold mines. It was during this period that my great-grandfather, fast asleep in his home, was woken suddenly in the depths of the night, instantly aware that something was amiss. He opened his eyes to discover that a criminal gang of Chinese men were in the process of breaking into his house in order to rob him.

The pioneering spirit was still alive and well in South Africa. All my great-grandfather had in hand as a weapon of self-defense, was a sword that he kept next to his bed. Snatching it up, he set about applying the business end of the sword to each robber, as each snuck into the house via the window. Details have become murky with the accumulation of intervening decades, but it seems that up to seven robbers were thus dispatched. Even though the odds were stacked heavily against him, my great-grandfather succeeded in overcoming and thwarting them.

What followed from this point is unclear, but one unsubstantiated rumor has it that one of the would-be robbers, in the process of escaping, may have delivered a curse on my great-grandfather and the generations of his family on that dark night long ago.

From time to time, when hardship and adversity and affliction and setback seem to flow in never-ending stream, the question comes up in the extended family, "Are we cursed?"

To answer this question, we need to take a look at what Scripture tells us on the subject.

The first matter to get out of the way immediately, is that God does not curse us. We are His dearly loved children, and His Word tells us that as such, His intentions toward us are always good, He is always working for our good, and He only ever does good to us:

*"For I know the plans I have for you," declares the Lord, "plans to prosper you and not to harm you, plans to give you hope and a future" (Jeremiah 29:11).*

*And we know that in all things God works for the good of those who love Him, who have been called according to His purpose (Romans 8:28).*

This leads us to the next question, and the one referred to earlier: what if someone else has "put a curse" on us?

Sadly, I know too many people living in fear and defeat because they believe this to be true. Evil certainly is a reality, and supernatural forces working for that evil, too, are real. It is also true that the "enemy of our souls" will attempt to oppose and oppress us, and that we will at times experience the effects of that opposition.

But oh, child of God, please hear me in this: There is no power in the universe greater than the power of God! When we are living our lives committed and surrendered to Him, no other power in the universe can prevail over or supersede or usurp His power at work in our lives! It is not a matter of a contest between two equally strong forces. God is without limit in His power and authority and majesty, and nothing that the enemy throws at us has any chance of succeeding when confronted with the power of God that rules and reigns in unsurpassed supremacy!

*"No weapon that is formed against you will succeed; And every tongue that rises against you in judgment you will condemn. This peace, righteousness, security, and triumph over opposition is the heritage of the servants of the Lord, and this is their vindication from Me" (Isaiah 54:17, Amplified Bible).*

In the Old Testament we read the story of Balaam, hired by King Balak, to put a curse on the Israelites. However, the Israelites were a people belonging to God. Consequently, no matter how much Balaam was paid to bring a curse against them, he was completely unable to do so. Their welfare and their future were entirely in the hands of God, and no matter how hard the enemy tried, he could not succeed in placing a curse where God had commanded blessing.

*Like a fluttering sparrow or a darting swallow, an underserved curse does not come to rest (Proverbs 26:2).*

*Devise your strategy, but it will be thwarted; propose your plan, but it will not stand, **for God is with us** (Isaiah 8:10).*

No power for evil can prevail against the power and purpose of God Almighty! At the end of Romans 8, the same chapter that tells us that God works all things together for our good, the Apostle Paul makes these further points:

*No, in all these things we are more than conquerors through Him who loved us (Romans 8:17).* The phrase "more than conquerors" is translated from the Greek compound word *hupernikos. Huper* means "way beyond measure, unsurpassed, unrivaled". *Nikos* means "conqueror, champion, victor, overwhelming prevailing force". Put these two words together, and the Bible tells us that because we live in the blessing of God's love we are "unequaled and unrivaled conquerors, an enormous conquering force"! The enemy is certainly not the one who holds the authority in our lives!

Paul then goes on to say that none of the following can separate us from that conquering love of God:

not death – meaning neither physical death nor life-threatening circumstances not life – including all the complex circumstances and issues of life

not angels – spiritual beings acting for good

not principalities – spiritual beings acting for evil

not powers – meaning the powerful governments of men

not height or depth – neither lofty or deep things

not any creature – anything in the created world, physical or spiritual

has the power or ability or capability to distance or disconnect you from the love of God in Christ Jesus, who is sovereign King of kings, ruling in and over my life and yours in all power and authority[13]! If you are living a life surrendered to Jesus Christ, there is no opportunity for any "curse" to take hold!

Several years ago I had a dream in which I had entered a small room, only to be confronted by an enormous, threatening "strongman". I knew that in my own strength I was too small and weak to overcome him. I also knew that if I turned and ran for the door in an effort to escape, he would be on me in a flash. In my heart I called out, "Jesus help me!" In that instant, Jesus appeared in the room, and He said, "Just stand right here". He positioned me beside Him, and slightly behind His right shoulder. Then He spoke just one word, and the "strongman" crumpled to the floor!

This is a wonderful picture of the supremacy of the power of Jesus in our lives when we remain positioned "in Him".

Another issue that is often raised, is that of "generational curses". In other words, the idea that because of the poor choices, lifestyle, and dysfunction of the generations before us, we continue to experience the "curse" of those consequences in our generation and in the generations that follow us. In support of this, the following is

[13]     "Sparkling Gems from the Greek", Rick Renner

quoted: "*The Lord is slow to anger, abounding in love and forgiving sin and rebellion. Yet He does not leave the guilty unpunished; He punishes the children for the sin of the parents to the third and fourth generation*" (Numbers 14:18).

The first problem with claiming that this passage speaks of "generational curse", is that it is quoted out of its context, and without regard to what the rest of Scripture has to say on the matter. Briefly, in other Scripture passages, for example Ezekiel 18, God clearly communicates that each person is accountable for his or her **own** sin, and that a child will not be punished for his parents' sin, or a parent for his child's sin. Additionally, the New Testament teaches that for those who surrender their lives to Jesus, they have been set free from condemnation!

*Therefore, there is now no condemnation for those who are in Christ Jesus, because through Christ Jesus the law of the Spirit who gives life has **set you free from the law of sin and death** (Romans 8:1, 2)*

What then, does the verse about punishing the children to the third and fourth generation actually mean? It simply refers to the natural law at work, that as parents, our poor choices and dysfunctional lifestyles have ongoing consequences in the lives of our children, and they in turn pass this learned behavior down to their children, and so on. We see this cycle most clearly in families afflicted by drug addiction or abusive patterns of behavior. Children are conditioned to repeat what has been modeled for them as they grow up, and they in turn pass the same down to their own children.

Through the generations then, the painful consequences of poor choices are lived out in a repetitious cycle of brokenness.

However, the Bible teaches us that this cycle of brokenness can be broken! You and I and our children and grandchildren can be set free!

*So if the Son sets you free, you will be **free indeed** (John 8:36).*

This is what this whole book has been about! God is not only able, but passionately invested, in redeeming, healing, restoring, and transforming all the brokenness that has come to you through the generations of your family. He can do what no other can do! He can break the chains of your past, bring wholeness to your present, and expectant hope to your future and that of your children and grandchildren.

See, there is another verse in the Old Testament that, strangely, often goes overlooked in any discussion on this topic. And it is this:

*"... but showing love to **a thousand generations** of those who love Me and keep My commandments" (Exodus 20:6).*

Generational blessing! If you come from generations of brokenness, and have committed your life to Jesus Christ, then not only does He redeem, heal and restore your own brokenness, but you now become the vehicle through whom He begins to release that same redemptive power to the generations of your family! Because of Jesus Christ in your life you are **blessed and carry blessing!**

The only way the old familiar destructiveness can take root is through your own choices and decisions. If you or I make destructive choices in and for our own lives, then we once again begin so sow seeds of destruction. God is not to blame for this; **we** have free will, and are accountable. But if we are willing to co-operate with Him, with the help and power of His Holy Spirit we are empowered to break free of the past.

We need to begin to declare the truth of God's Word over our own lives. Revelation 12:11 has these powerful words: *They* (believers) *overcame him* (the enemy) *by the blood of the Lamb* (Jesus) *and by the word of their testimony; they did not love their lives so much as to shrink from death.*

The "word of their testimony" in this passage refers to what we say about Jesus. Instead of saying "I'm cursed" or "our family is cursed", we should be saying, "I am a child of God, bought with the blood of Jesus. He is Lord of my life, and has all power, all authority in my life. I am a conqueror in Him, and He is working all things for good in my life. I am blessed because I'm His child. He is redeeming and restoring and transforming every lost and broken and wounded thing, and I am free indeed because of Him!"

Let us stop claiming curses for our lives, and instead keep *fixing our eyes on Jesus, the author and perfecter of our faith (Hebrews 12:2).*

*The Lord will perfect that which concerns me… (Psalm 138:8).*

*The One who calls you is faithful, and He will do it (1 Thessalonians 5:24).*

*Praise be to the God and Father of our Lord Jesus Christ, who has blessed us in the heavenly realms with every spiritual blessing in Christ (Ephesians 1:3).*

## What About You?

1. Have you been in fear that there might be a "curse" operating over your life for one reason or another?

2. Pray: Thank the Lord for His completed work on the cross. Thank Him that His work on the cross has broken all the power of the enemy over your life. Thank Him that He rules in love, authority, and power in your life, and is at work in and through your life to heal, redeem and restore. Claim the truth of His Word over your own life and the lives of your family members – that He is at work to bring blessing to the generations of your family.

3 If you carry personal wounds resulting from broken and dysfunctional family experiences, seek out a Christian counselor who can minister to you in prayer, and in the wisdom and power of the Holy Spirit.

# CHAPTER 18
# IS YOUR LAZARUS DEAD?

*E*xperience tells me that even having read all of the above, there will still be some whose response is, "It's too late for me. I've prayed and waited and hoped and believed, and now it is too late…"

*"Woman, why are you weeping?" (John 20:13, 15).*

These are the words that Jesus spoke outside the empty tomb, to a weeping Mary Magdalene.

In fact, a study of the original language in this passage reveals that Mary Magdalene was not just weeping - she was sobbing. She was grief-stricken and heart broken and distraught. So much so, that when she turned around and saw Jesus standing there, and He asked her the same question the angels had asked, *"Woman, why are you weeping?"* she did not even recognize Him. Until He spoke her name…

*"Mary."*

When she heard His voice speak her name in this personal and intimate way, she recognized the presence of her beloved Lord. In that moment, everything changed.

The question that is burning in my heart for you, dear reader, is "Why are **you** weeping?" What circumstances, what experiences, what absence, what emptiness, what pain has left you grief-stricken and heart-broken, your heart sobbing in agony, "Where is He? I don't know where He is!"

Oh He has been there all along, dear ones, but in your stricken and distraught state, you have not recognized His near presence in your circumstances.

To each one of you whose heart is right now broken and crying out in pain and sorrow, my prayer for you, is this: I pray in the name of the One who loves you with a deep and inexhaustible love, that today, even as you read this, you will hear your Lord speaking your name as personally and intimately as He called Mary's that day. And as you hear His voice speak your name, may your eyes be opened to recognize the presence of Him whose love never fails, never wearies, never falls short - and holds you all the days of your life.

Not too many weeks before this encounter outside the empty tomb, Jesus approached another tomb, and spoke with another Mary, and her sister Martha. The story is told in John 11. In some ways, they could not understand why He had even bothered coming at all, since it was too late anyway. Lazarus was dead. In fact, he had been dead four days

As unmarried women, Lazarus was more than Mary and Martha's closest family: he was also their only means of provision for their lives and their future. When Lazarus died, hope died. We hear their despair and underlying accusation in their words, individually and separately, to Jesus, *"Lord, if only you had been here, our brother would not have died."*

"Lord, if only You had answered when I first prayed, when I first asked, this would not have happened. Lord, didn't You care enough to answer me when I first cried out to You? Now it is too late."

Are these not the kinds of words that echo in our own hearts, even if we dare not say them out loud?

It is fascinating to witness the response of Jesus when He first learned of Lazarus' serious illness: *"This sickness will not **end** in death. No, it is for God's glory..." Jesus **loved** Martha and her sister and Lazarus ... when He heard that Lazarus was sick, He **stayed where He was two more days** (John 11:4-6).*

Only after Lazarus had already died, did Jesus respond and begin the 21-mile journey on foot from the Jordan to Bethany of Judea. He had not been very far away all along! Nevertheless, the road led through mountainous terrain, and so it was another two days before He finally arrived in Bethany. Martha and Mary's bewilderment at His apparently deliberate delay echo through the words with which they greet Him – the same words that become our own refrain:

"If only..."

But Jesus responds to Martha and Mary's "if only" – and to my "if only" and yours – with these words: *"I AM the resurrection and the life..." (John 11:25).*

How those words resonate in my own heart! Mary and Martha discovered that day what Job had discovered centuries before: The answer to the death of our "Lazarus" lies in **who Jesus is.** What we need more than anything at such times, is a fresh revelation to our hearts, of who He is in His being, in His essence, in His character, in His power and authority.

Job responded to just such a revelation with these words: *"My ears had heard of You but now my eyes have seen You. Therefore I... repent in dust and ashes" (Job 42:5, 6).*

Jesus wept at the tomb of Lazarus, and I believe this has frequently been misinterpreted: He did not weep because Lazarus was dead. Death was no deterrent to "The Resurrection and the Life". I believe He wept both because of the sin and resulting suffering in fallen humanity, and because of our incomprehension of and lack of belief in who He is. *"He who **believes** in Me will live... Do **you believe** this?" (John 11:25, 26).*

The Greek word used of Martha and Mary weeping signify sobbing; the word used of Jesus weeping is a different one, indicating silent tears rolling down His cheeks.

As Jesus' tears dried, He called out in the voice of the authority and power of The Resurrection and the Life: *"Lazarus, come out!"*

That voice penetrated the grave and broke the chains of death and raised a four-day corpse to renewed life! Lazarus' sickness did not **end** in death! It led **through** death to end in supernatural victory!

Cultural tradition had it that the spirit of the deceased hovered about the body for three days following death – so that in the minds of the people, it may yet be within the realm of possibility for a corpse to be revived within the first three days. By the fourth day, however, it was believed that the spirit had departed altogether, and that there remained no possibility of resuscitation.

Jesus' seemingly incomprehensible delay was Divinely intentional: Jesus' raising of Lazarus testified to His Divine, supernatural power that accomplishes miracles in the face of the humanly impossible.

*"Did I not tell you that if you believed, you would see the glory of God?" (Luke 11:40)*

Is your "Lazarus" dead? What hope has died in your life? What bewilderment has assailed your heart because it feels that when you called on the Lord for His intervention and help, there seemed to be no response, and now it is "too late"? What "Lazarus" of yours seems now beyond the reach of all help?

When you stand alongside Jesus at the tomb of your dead Lazarus, who then, do **you** say that He is?

"I AM the Resurrection and the Life!" Do **you** believe this?

In the place of your "impossible" and your "too late", I pray this for you:

- I pray that you will receive a fresh revelation to your own heart, of who Jesus is.
- I pray that your belief in Him who is The Resurrection and the Life will rise to stand with Him at the tomb of your "Lazarus".
- I pray that the glory of God and the God of glory will be demonstrated in the very place of your deepest hopelessness.
- I pray that the voice of the One who raised Lazarus and was Himself resurrected from the dead not many weeks following, will reverberate with undeniable authority, calling your dead

hopes, dreams, relationships, purpose, calling — and any other "death" - back to life.

- I pray that faith will rise to say, with Job, *"I know that You can do all things; no plan of Yours can be thwarted" (Job 42:2)*.

- I pray that whatever has seemed to thwart your life's hope, will not **end** in "death", but will lead **through** "death" to resound with supernatural victory in Him who holds all power, all authority, and all life!

Why are **you** weeping?

Insert your name here, as these words echo in your own desperate heart: "_____ *why are you weeping?"*

Pour out your heart to Him - all your deepest fears and sorrows. And then turn and hear as He speaks your name: "_____"

He is the One poured out in love and resurrected in power to redeem all that you surrender at His nail-scarred feet. Your Lazarus may well be dead, but your Jesus is the Resurrection and the Life, and the Power and the Wisdom of God (1 Corinthians 1:24)!

<u>**What About You?**</u>

1. Does it feel to you as if God's answer to your prayers is too late, and now all that you hoped and prayed for is beyond redemption?

2. I pray that you will take the hand of Jesus, and stand with Him at the tomb of your buried hopes and dreams. I pray that His voice will resound through all your circumstances and experiences, and into eternity, "Come forth!" I pray that the Resurrection and the Life will redeem and restore every God-given, divine, sovereign purpose that He holds in His heart for you. I pray that out of the ashes, a beauty will arise that radiates with the glory of God and the God of glory!

# PRAYER

*I*f material trash, in the hands of African people, can be transformed into that which is so good and beautiful and unique that visitors come from all over the world to buy it, can you just imagine what our personal "trash" could become in the hands of the Creator of all the universe?

The experiences and circumstances in life that seem the trashiest of all, are the very things that will shine with the radiance of God's beauty and splendor when given into His hands.

Are you tired of carrying trash around, tired of trying to live past or around the trash of your personal life? The trash of loss, of broken relationships, of mistakes made, of injustices suffered… Whether it is trash from thirty years ago, or trash from last year, or trash from last week or yesterday or even today, Jesus invites you to open up the dark closet in your heart, and allow Him to take the trash hidden there in His hands. Then watch what happens as in those hands, it is transformed into…

something useful…

something lovely…

something that produces a beautiful sound and a sweet fragrance from your life…

something radiant with the glory of God…

Do you long for God to turn the "trash" of your life, into treasure? Is it your desire to open the door of that dark closet in your life and invite Him in to transform it into something that radiates with His light, is filled with His purpose, brings forth a captivating sound and releases a sweet fragrance?

Yet another of my favorite songs, by a group called Gungor, is titled "Beautiful Things". The lyrics of this song wonderfully capture the message of the book you hold in your hands:

All this pain
I wonder if I'll ever find my way
I wonder if my life could really change at all
All this earth
Could all that is lost ever be found
Could a garden come up from this ground at all

All around
Hope is springing up from this old ground
Out of chaos life is being found in You

You make beautiful things
You make beautiful things out of the dust
You make beautiful things
You make beautiful things out of us

You make me new, You are making me new
You make me new, You are making me new

Very often I express my own prayers in the form of poetry. You can pray the following prayer-poem with me, but I also urge you to continue looking to the One who is Redeemer and Restorer, and to continue lifting your own heart of prayer to Him in your own words:

### Alabastar Jar

This broken vessel,
Lord, I lay
At Your scarred feet,
Where shattered shards
Of splintered heart
And Your great mercy
Meet.

This alabaster
Jar that held
Life's woken dreams —
In ruins now —
Each piece I place
Where nail-pierced grace
Redeems.

Release sweet fragrance

Lord, I pray,

Costly though it be,

From life poured out

Of brokenness

Surrendered, Lord,

To Thee.

Avril VanderMerwe

©2001

# APPENDIX

There are numerous tools and resources available that provide help to those seeking to live restored, transformed lives. One such recently published resource is a book called *Growing Sronger: 12 Guidelines Designed to Turn Your Darkest Hour into Your Greatest Victory* by Mary Beth Woll and Paul Meier.

As previously mentioned, I also strongly recommend the books and resources of Dr. Caroline Leaf.

I may also be reached via my Facebook ministry page at https://www.facebook.com/avril.isaiah58.12/

CPSIA information can be obtained
at www.ICGtesting.com
Printed in the USA
BVHW01s2209010118
504153BV00001B/148/P